THE FICTION AND CRITICISM

OF

KATHERINE ANNE PORTER

by

Harry John Mooney, Jr.

Number Two

Critical Essays in English and American Literature

UNIVERSITY OF PITTSBURGH PRESS

PITTSBURGH: 1957

LIBRARY OF CONGRESS CATALOG CARD NUMBER: 57-9404

© 1957 University of Pittsburgh Press

Printed in U.S.A.

THE TEXT IS SET IN LINOTYPE CALEDONIA; THE
DISPLAY TYPE, IN BULMER. THE BOOK IS PRINTED
ON WARREN'S OLDE STYLE ANTIQUE WHITE WOVE
PAPER, BY WILLIAM G. JOHNSTON COMPANY OF
PITTSBURGH. IT IS PUBLISHED BY THE UNIVERSITY
OF PITTSBURGH PRESS, PITTSBURGH, PA.

THE FICTION AND CRITICISM
OF KATHERINE ANNE PORTER

Katherine Anne Porter is an anomaly in contemporary American literature. The amount of her published work is very small, and her reputation is extremely high with nearly all schools of modern critics. But, to some extent at least, her sucess has been largely critical; she has never had the popular acclaim of Ernest Hemingway or even William Faulkner. Her lack of general popularity is no doubt partly attributable to the fact that she has chosen to work in two of the forms with which the reading public has least patience: the short story and its cousin, the *nouvelle*. All of Miss Porter's fiction has been collected in three books: *Flowering Judas and Other Stories* (originally published in 1930, and republished, with four additional stories, in 1935), *Pale Horse, Pale Rider* (1939), and *The Leaning Tower and Other Stories* (1944). One other book, *The Days Before*, a collection of essays and occasional pieces, appeared in 1952. For some time Miss Porter has been engaged in writing a novel, to be entitled *No Safe Harbor*, four fragments of which have appeared in *Harper's Magazine* during the last four years.

Miss Porter's work has been praised for various reasons, but mainly for its high level of technical accomplishment in matters of style, form, precision, and so on. Too often, reviewers and serious critics alike have stressed these qualities in her writing at the expense of its substance, and the extraordinary unity of meaning and feeling in her prose has been almost ignored. Style and form, in Miss Porter's fiction, represent the most direct means to a given end: rendering a particular facet of human life in an attempt to arrive at its significance. Miss Porter does not, so far as I can see, experiment with forms or techniques, and her style in one story is a good deal like her style in another, though, of course, its tone may and frequently does change. But she represents, as she herself indicates in numerous passages in *The Days Before*, the kind of writer who has something to say rather than the writer who consciously strives for perfection of style or form. The clarity of her style and the precision of her language add greatly to the power of what she has to say, of course, but it is the meaning of human experience as she visualizes it which is of most significance.

Perhaps the most baffling thing of all about Miss Porter's achievement is its nearly incredible consistency; both lesser and greater writers may be approached through their faults or through their deflections from recognized standards. Miss Porter, however, is nearly faultless within the limits of her work: were her output broader, she might well be the foremost writer on the American scene. Some of the statements in *The Days Before* relate the limitations of her work to the history of her age, and this is not unlikely. For, first and foremost, Miss Porter writes as a woman of her particular time, a witness of a special kind of human experience as well as of a unique and terrible chapter in the history of mankind. Her fiction reveals a consistent vision of the issues of the present age, dramatized and given meaning through the meaning of her art. It is the purpose of this paper to indicate what that meaning is, and to examine those particular kinds of experience in which Miss Porter seems most interested and which form the central patterns of her work.

PROFILE OF AN ARTIST

In 1944, when Katherine Anne Porter published her third volume of short stories, *The Leaning Tower and Other Stories*, Edmund Wilson wrote a criticism of the book, or, more particularly, of its author, for *The New Yorker* magazine.[1] Wilson's article was not in the best tradition of his work, since he confessed at the outset that Miss Porter's fiction confounded him "because one cannot take hold of [it] in any of the obvious ways. She makes none of the melodramatic or ironic points that are the stock in trade of ordinary short-story writers; she falls into none of the usual patterns and she does not show anyone's influence." Then, after attempting to group the stories and novelettes according to their settings and subject matter, Wilson goes on, "But I am spoilng Miss Porter's stories by attempting to find a formula for them when I ought simply to be telling you to read them. . . . She is absolutely a first-rate artist, and what she wants other people to know she imparts to them by creating an object, the self-developing organism of a work of prose." And he concludes his estimate by quoting from Miss Porter's preface to *Flowering Judas*, as being "more to the purpose than anything that the present critic could say."

Stanley Edgar Hyman later made use of this article in his attack on Wilson,[2] and claimed that it represented a deliberate "abdication of the critical function." But I suspect this is not quite fair, for one must take into account the fact that none of our eminent contemporary critics of any school has successfully elucidated, or even written about, Miss Porter's work. Each of them seems to content himself with short statements of the highest praise containing no specific critical analysis. Why is this so? What is the element in her work that leads her to be praised so extravagently, and even to the invidious designation of being "a writer's writer," at the same time that no really fresh light is thrown on the meaning and development of her art? Why is indiscriminate praise, and this only, the particular portion of this extraordinary American writer?

Since Mr. Wilson wrote his article, nearly a decade has elapsed, and we are now in a better positon to answer some of these questions, for in the interval Katherine Anne Porter has published *The Days Before*, her own book of essays, sketches and critical pieces. Where our critics have failed, Miss Porter herself has sometimes, but not always, succeeded in analyzing her position in respect to English and American letters and to society and its larger problems. Furthermore, the tone of the book is so personal that one gets a kind of self-portrait as well, a revelation of opinions, impressions and ideas proceeding directly from the writer.

Why does Miss Porter write? She tells us, succinctly and eloquently, in the preface to which Mr. Wilson had recourse, and which she reprints in *The Days Before*. This preface, only two paragraphs in length, was written in the June of 1940, just ten days after the fall of Paris. It was designed for the Modern Library edition of *Flowering Judas*, Miss Porter's first collection of stories. Its grasp of the special dilemma of twentieth century writer reveals its author as a woman of her age, full of faith, hope and courage, and far removed from any ivory tower:

It is just ten years since this collection of short stories first appeared. They are literally first fruits, for they were written and published in order of their present arrangement in this volume, which contains the first story I ever finished. Looking at them again, it is possible still to say that I do not repent of them; if they were not yet written, I should have to write them still. They were done with intention and in firm faith, though I had no plan for their future and no notion of what their meaning might be to such readers as they would find. To any speculations from interested sources as to why there were not more of them I can answer simply and truthfully that I was not one of those who could flourish in the conditions of the last two decades. They are fragments of a much larger plan which I am still engaged in carrying out, and they are what I was then able to achieve in the way of order and form and statement in a period of grotesque dislocations in a whole society when the world was heaving in the sickness of a millennial change. They were first published by what seems still merely a lucky accident, and their survival through this crowded and slowly darkening decade is the sort of fate no one, least of all myself, could be expected to predict or even to hope for.

We none of us flourished in those times, artists or not, for art, like the human life of which it is the truest voice, thrives best by daylight in a green and growing world. For myself, and I was not alone, all the conscious and recollected years of my life have been lived to this day under the heavy threat of world catastrophe, and most of the energies of my mind and spirit have been spent in the effort to grasp the meaning of those threats, to trace them to their sources and to understand the logic of this majestic and terrible failure of the life of man in the Western world. In the face of such shape and weight of present misfortune, the voice of an individual artist may seem perhaps of no more consequence than the whirring of a cricket in the grass; but the arts do live continuously and they live literally by faith; their names and their shapes and their uses and their basic meanings survive unchanged in all that matters through times of interruption, diminishment, neglect; they outlive governments and creeds and the societies, even the very civilization that produced them. They cannot be destroyed altogether because they represent the substance of faith and the only reality. They are what we find again when the ruins are cleared away. And even the smallest and most incomplete offering at this time can be a proud act in defense of that faith.[3]

This is Miss Porter's statement of her faith in the continuity of the arts and in their deep relevancy to the human situation in any age. But this is only the superstructure of her thinking in this matter; what also emerges clearly from the above is that she writes as any true artist must, out of deep inner necessity. This necessity, however, has purpose and direction: it seeks to trace the reasons for the failures of man's behavior in our time, and so Miss Porter's stories are studies in concrete and specific instances of human behavior. Queerly enough, and in spite of all the praise lavished on her style, her technique, her form, and her creation of atmosphere, even her friendliest critics seem to have missed the actual pivot of all her fiction: the diverse and baffling conduct of man. That so much praise has so consistently gone wide of its mark is possibly an indication of the division between the life of literature and the critics who attempt to elucidate it.

The second most important point in Miss Porter's preface lies in her remark that her stories are "fragments of a much larger plan which I am still engaged in carrying out." All three of her books of stories are thus parts of one long work; and each story, representing one particular facet of human behavior, is a small part of one large organic whole. Somewhere in the midst of these stories, and I suspect that even Miss Porter herself could not be explicit as to just *where*, lie the indications of man's moral and intellectual failures. As a true representative of her age, Miss Porter is compelled to write about a society that is haunted from within and threatened from without. Like Henry James, whom she greatly admires, she has the "imagination of disaster," the particular hallmark of the literary artist in America which runs from Hawthorne and Melville, through James, to Fitzgerald and Faulkner and Hemingway. Miss Porter's apprehension of catastrophe seems not altogether a part of her equipment as an artist; much of it seems a complement of her sense of history. And nowhere does she state her premonitions as clearly as James consistently does; none of her stories leads to a climax as horrifying as James's *The Beast in the Jungle* or *The Turn of the Screw*, for example. Because her sense of evil is less specific, she has dramatized it in smaller symbols, like the little plaster cast of the Leaning Tower of Pisa, which, in the story *The Leaning Tower*, appears at first to be merely a part of the bric-a-brac surrounding the German landlady but which somehow translates itself into a dynamic symbol of the whole rotten structure of German political society about to collapse before the rising tide of Nazism.

From Miss Porter's statements in *The Days Before*, as well as from the clarity and impact of her stories themselves, her purpose in writing fiction should be clear. It is the psychology of human relations which interests her most, and each of her stories is an attempt to elucidate some particular problem or mystery in man's behavior. And, like all true artists, she succeeds so well because she frequently illuminates the human situation in a way that seems wholly new to us. Most of her stories deal with the failure of love or hope or fortitude, and in this they reflect not only the contemporary, but the ageless, dilemmas. But against these stories, we have another kind which give us a kind of counterpoint in theme. This second group is comprised of the stories set in an older world of known and stable values, a world where a certain right to egoism may nearly be taken for granted. I refer especially to the first six sketches in *The Leaning Tower*, each of them a brilliant evocation of the childhood of Miranda, who lives in the quick responsive atmosphere of innocence, wrapped round by the safe, happy, sound enough values of the last of the Southern pioneer aristocrats. Nonetheless, the world of Miranda's childhood is foredoomed by the rapidity of industrial expansion, and we have only to turn to *Old Mortality* and *Pale Horse, Pale Rider*, the first and third novelettes in the book *Pale Horse, Pale Rider*, to learn how painfully Miranda comes to maturity in the knowledge of her family and of war and of disappointed love. Miranda thus moves between the two poles consistently observed in all Miss Porter's work: the safe world of illusion and youth and innocence and the hard and actual world of maturity and disillusion and a hard-won fortitude.

Miranda, appearing as she does in two of Miss Porter's three books of fiction and in eight of her twenty-two published stories, marks the closest approach we have to a central character in the work as a whole. And, while it would be rash to say that she represents Miss Porter herself, one can safely assume that she is her most subjective creation and that she at least approximates some aspects of Miss Porter's personal history. Like her creator, Miranda passes her childhood in the twilight world of the old South at the turn of the century (Miss Porter substantiates her own similar background in *The Days Before* in a short piece called *Portrait: Old South*, almost identical in atmosphere and detail with the six sketches from *The Leaning Tower*), and, again like the author, she comes to maturity just before and during the first World War. Miss Porter herself once observed that she did cherish one of her longer stories above anything else she had ever written, though for "extremely personal reasons," and one is tempted to speculate that the story must be *Pale Horse, Pale Rider*, especially since, in the same interview, Miss Porter admitted that Miranda's experience with illness and her presentiments of death derived from her own experience during the influenza epidemic of 1918.[4] Miranda's history is characteristic of Miss Porter's work: it has the universality of all her stories and yet it is splendidly specific in treatment; it represents the particular dramatized in terms of the general.

In *The Days Before*, however, we have no need to speculate about *alter egos*, since, much of the time, Miss Porter is being brilliantly herself. In her preface to the book, she writes that she likes to think of it as a kind of journal of her thirty developing years as a published writer, and she hopes that the reader will find in it, "the shape, direction, and connective tissue of a continuous, central interest and preoccupation of a lifetime." And, barring some occasional but appalling slips from a high standard (which led Mark Schorer to comment, in *The New Republic*, on the polish and lucidity of most of the essays in contrast to the "vulgarity" of some of the others, like the one on the rose, written for the highly commercial and now defunct periodical, *Flair*), *The Days*

Before achieves its stated purpose. And the dichotomy apparent in these essays may be accounted for by Miss Porter's note, in her foreward, on her methods as a writer:

They (the essays) represent the exact opposite of my fiction, in that they were written nearly all by request, with limitations of space, a date fixed for finishing, on a chosen subject or theme, as well as with the certainty that they would be published. I wrote as well as I could at any given moment under a variety of pressures, and said what I meant as nearly as I could come to it: so as they stand, the pieces are all parts of a journal of my thinking and feeling. . . . My stories had to be accepted and published exactly as they were written: that rule has never once been broken. There was no one, whose advice I respected, whose help I would not have been glad to get, and many times did get, on almost any of these articles. I have written, re-written, and revised them. My stories, on the other hand, are written in one draft, and if short enough, at one sitting. In fact, this book would seem to represent the other half of a double life: but not in truth. It is all one thing. The two ways of working helped and supported each other: I needed both.[5]

Furthermore, the uneven quality of these essays is at least partly attributable to the variety of subjects with which they deal. Some of them, like *A House of One's Own,* which is an account of Miss Porter's search for the particular kind of house she had always visualized, are charming but too capricious to be significant. Two essays on marriage are an odd mixture of the intelligent and the sententious. And some of the comments on other writers and their works betray an uncomfortably seignorial tone. Much of this can be overlooked, however, in favor of those other parts of *The Days Before* which give us the most cherished convictions of a major artist expressed with the utmost clarity. These passages from the book, and they are numerous, provide a clear insight into the kind of intellectual framework that underlies the stories themselves.

The first section of *The Days Before,* labelled *Critical,* opens with a fairly long and beautifully written essay on Henry James (the title piece in the volume), which confines itself to an evocation of the atmosphere of the master's childhood and education, and which, firmly though it establishes its mood and sustains the quality of its prose, manages somehow to say very little that is new and leaves the impression of a minor excursion into the period piece. Miss Porter uses as epigraph for this piece a critical comment by James now rendered famous in many connections, but which is obviously relevant to her own concept of her art: "Really, universally, relations stop nowhere, and the exquisite problem of the artist is eternally but to draw, by a geometry of his own, the circle within which they shall happily *appear* to do so."[6] This remark connects directly with the fragmentary principle so obviously limiting Miss Porter's own work, and it seems to entitle us to suggest that the only "circle" within which, for her, relations might "appear" to end, particularly in this threatened mid-century, must of necessity be that of the short, the rounded, the pointed. The world of the last sixty years, Miss Porter's lifetime, with its two world wars, totalitarian phantoms, disease, famine, strife and increasingly limited human freedom, presents itself to the artist more and more in chaotic, broken forms. Miss Porter herself admits in the preface already quoted, that she was not one of those who could "flourish" in such a period, and, in another essay which served originally as an introduction to Eudora Welty's first book, she vigorously defends the legitimacy of the short story and the right of the writer to choose the form in which he is most congenial. The "circle" for Miss Porter has not been the novel, but the short or long story, and sometimes merely the sketch.

Miss Porter returns frequently, in *The Days Before,* to James, who evidently occupies for her the most luminous position in our literature. She reprints her answers to seven questions sent out to some American writers and philosophers by the *Partisan Review* in 1939. One question, "Would you say, for example, that Henry James's work is more relevant to the present and future of American writing than Walt Whitman's?" draws the answer that discriminations of this kind are beside the point, since both men are salient in our literary history. But Miss Porter continues:

For myself, I choose James, holding as I do with the conscious disciplined artist, the serious expert against the expansive, indiscriminately "cosmic" sort. James, I believe, was the better workman, the more advanced craftsman, a better thinker, a man with a heavier load to carry than Whitman. His feelings are deeper and more complex than Whitman's; he had more confusing choices to make, he faced and labored over broader problems.[7]

Now the connection between the aims of James and that of Miss Porter herself is obvious here. She tells us that she admires his ability as a *craftsman;* that his feelings were more *complex* than Whitman's; that he made *choices* and labored over harder *problems;* and, most important of all, that he represents what Miss Porter believes in, "the consciously *disciplined* artist." What James achieved, in other words, was a lucidity of expression, a compactness of form, based on choice and discipline and the determination to solve the most difficult problems of his craft. By this process, he was able to illuminate the most complex situations and to present them in an order and logic imposed by his consciousness of the functions of his art. The underlined words in Miss Porter's appreciation of James establish the nature of his influence on her, and tell us something about the services she belives he renders to the writers of our own time. Like Henry James, Miss Porter works hardest, I believe, on form, so that her impressions of a chaotic world apparently in the process of falling to pieces before her, are given meaning and clarity by the order of their presentation. Now style, with Miss Porter as with James, is the direct result of the discipline that only form can impose; and Miss Porter's language, again like James's, represents an effort to find the most direct and precise method of presenting emotional effects. James, however, was to find emotional processes so subtle and complicated that his style grew steadily more shaded and obscure; whereas Miss Porter has kept her language as simple as possible for any given situation. The result has been that she writes an English of such purity that she has come to be, in Edmund Wilson's words, "almost unique in contemporary American literature."[8] Because of this, the attention of her readers has been drawn to diction when it often might have been more properly directed to form. And the entire connection between Katherine Anne Porter and Henry James rests on the sense of form, the determination to present situations and relations as effectively as possible.

Miss Porter writes in another context in *The Days Before:* "I agree with E. M. Forster that there are only two possibilities for any real order: in art and in religion."[9] This, taken together with her confession in the preface to *Flowering Judas*, should make clear the purpose of her work. She is attempting, in all her stories, to render intelligible the chaos of the present age, "the majestic and terrible failure of the life of man in the Western world," by means of the order and form which only art (or religion) can achieve. Since that form has inevitably been, for Miss Porter at least, the short or long story, the question is only how well she has worked within this form, and not why she has never written a novel, a question which some supplement reviewers idly persist in asking.

Miss Porter includes an appreciation of Ezra Pound in *The Days Before*, in which she remembers a conversation between herself and Hart Crane. Crane had exclaimed, "I'm tired of Ezra Pound!" and Miss Porter had replied, "But who else is there?" And she goes on to say that most of the writers who came to maturity at the time of herself and Crane (between, roughly, 1910 and 1920) were "educated, you might say, in contemporary literature, not at schools at all but by five writers: Henry James, James Joyce, W. B. Yeats, T. S. Eliot, and Ezra Pound."[10] Then, in a short piece on Virginia Woolf, Miss Porter adds the name of the British novelist to the list: "She was one of the writers who touched the real life of my mind and feeling very deeply; I had from that book *(The Voyage Out)* the same sense of some mysterious revelation of truth I had got in earliest youth from Laurence Sterne, from Jane Austen, from Emily Bronte, from Henry James. I had grown up with these, and I went on growing with W. B. Yeats, the first short stories of James Joyce, the earliest novels of Virginia Woolf."[11] The list, it will be noted, is quite representative; one has only to add the name of Joseph Conrad to complete the roster of those British and American writers who shaped most decisively the course of English literature during the years 1880-1925.

Miss Porter makes another comment on Virginia Woolf which perhaps points up an awareness of her own limitations: "She lived in the naturalness of her vocation. The world of the arts was her native territory; she ranged freely under her own sky, speaking her mother tongue fearlessly. She was at home in that place as much as anyone ever was."[12] Because of this, Virginia Woolf's career shows a consecutive development and unfolding of her artistic powers. But this has not been true of Miss Porter, who seems to represent, in contrast to the private writer, the writer with a public conscience, harassed and interrupted by the history of her age, and thus prevented from reaching the potential peak of her achievement. If this be so, and I think it is, her career, as well as her fragmentary output, underlines the personal tragedy of the writer of sensibility sometimes rendered powerless by the overpowering currents of contemporary history. She has had, all along, and she discloses in *The Days Before*, such an acute sense of history, general and particular, that her work has far more relevance to the human situation than that of any mere "stylist" (a designation usually used in the pejorative sense) could command. Her talent is not robust, and she does not, of course, write about the public personages or the great events of her age. She deals solely with the depths and enigmas of human relations as they present themselves to her, and always, beneath the surface of any given story, lies the attempt to find the reasons for the present failure of human life. Unlike a writer like Sinclair Lewis, who went on publishing long after he had nothing to say, she has published only what she considers the best of her work. The result has presented the critics with a dilemma: a writer who has never published anything that may ultimately be judged weak or bad.

The critical section of *The Days Before* has a very narrow range, and the essays in it are confined to a comparatively small group of writers. Miss Porter has nothing to say about either classical or continental literature, but devotes herself rigorously to the English literature of the last seventy-five years, and along the lines of those authors already indicated. Miss Porter makes it clear to any reader who are the writers who have most affected her. There is a fairly long essay on Thomas Hardy, one of the most formal and eloquent in the entire book, which somewhat surprisingly, in view of Miss Porter's other stated preferences, defends him against his present detractors. In concluding her Hardy essay, Miss Porter stresses some of the qualities she admires in James, and we can see how Hardy, too, is related to the organic principles on which her own art is based: "By his own testimony, he limited his territory by choice, set boundaries to his material, focused his point of view like a burning glass on a definite aspect of things. He practiced a stringent discipline, severely excised and eliminated all that seemed to him not useful or appropriate to his plan. In the end his work was the sum of his experience, he arrived at his particular true testimony; along the way, sometimes, many times, he wrote sublimely."[13] Miss Porter herself has achieved her own "particular true testimony" by similar processes of elimination and discipline.

Following the Hardy essay in *The Days Before* are three views of

Gertrude Stein, written in 1927, 1928, and 1947. The first two are fragmentary and of no particular value except as they prepare us for the third. This third view, *The Wooden Umbrella*, is the longest essay in the critical section of the book next to the one on Henry James. It is by far the most trenchantly thought out and stated; its tone is a masterful and sustained mixture of levity and high seriousness, dignity and caprice; and it succeeds so well in stating Miss Porter's devastating view of Gertrude Stein that, to my mind at least, it appears to be the best essay in the entire book. Deftly and surely, Miss Porter strips away layer after layer of the famous Stein legend and reveals the void at its center. With some biographical annotation and careful arrangement of its material, with its presentation of a view of Gertrude Stein in concrete, factual terms, *The Wooden Umbrella* satirizes beautifully the kind of writer who operates in a moral vacuum, dealing solely with words and technical innovations, and completely devoid of feeling for, and contact with, the living.

Another of the best essays in *The Days Before* is one entitled simply, *Reflections on Willa Cather*. This, like the Stein essay, is an illustration of impressionostic criticism at its best. Here the material is organized around one central theme: Willa Cather's hardihood, her ability to endure the most abrupt changes in fashion, to state simply the true and the profound and thus achieve the timeless. During Willa Cather's lifetime, Miss Porter writes, "Sigmund Freud happened," Stravinsky happened," and "James Joyce happened," but Willa Cather worked on persistently, holding to her methods and beliefs as firmly as a life-raft, citing the "Hebrew prophets, the Greek dramatists, Goethe, Shakespeare, Dante, Tolstoy, Flaubert."[14] Speaking of Maxwell Geismar's including Willa Cather in a book of criticism called *The Last of the Provincials*, Miss Porter believes that he has a case, although she has not read his book: "Indeed, Willa Cather was as provincial as Hawthorne or Flaubert or Turgenev, as little concerned with aesthetics and as much with morals as Tolstoy, as obstinately reserved as Melville. In fact she always reminds me of very good literary company, of the particularly admirable company who formed her youthful tastes, her thinking and feeling."[15] By holding to these masters, in other words, Willa Cather survived in a period of flux; her career is at the opposite pole from those of Joyce, James, Virginia Woolf and the other writers whose innovations in style and form and method transformed the literature of the English language.

The rest of the critical pieces in *The Days Before* are shorter, less substantial and more superficial; some of them show the limitations of the media for which they were written, particularly the brief pieces which appeared originally in *The New York Times Book Review*. Three of these last, on Virginia Woolf, Ford Madox Ford, and E. M. Forster, are in the nature of tributes to accepted masters, but each of them is freshly written and bears its author's personal stamp in its clear insights into the beliefs and faiths underlying the work of these writers. Miss Porter writes, for example, of E. M. Forster:

He pokes fun at things in themselves fatally without humor, things oppressive and fatal to human happiness: megalomania, solemn-godliness, pretentiousness, self-love, the meddlesome impulse which leads to the invasion and destruction of human rights. He disclaims a belief in Belief, meaning one can only suppose the kind of dogmatism promoted by meddlesomeness and the rest; come right down to it, I hardly know a writer with more beliefs than Mr. Forster; and all on the side of the angels.[16]

The last sentence here indicates Miss Porter's particular method of impressionistic criticism: she seems to be thinking her way through her material as she writes. This is probably why the prose of the essays, though usually on the same high level as that of the fiction, is somewhat more mannered, depending often on eccentric punctuation and odd rhythms which appear to carry out the thinking process within the sentence itself.

The same quick perception which Miss Porter turns on E. M. Forster operates in many of the critical essays. Here is an artist's intuition supplying the missing data in the letters of Rainer Maria Rilke:

He depended in all faith and with good reason, too, on the tenderness and sympathy of women: all of them high-minded, romantic, and some of them very gifted, many nobly born and wealthy: but, alas, seekers after the man-god rather than the God in man.[17]

Here the impressions are compressed by the punctuation into one sentence, and the colons are used to show how one thought leads logically to the next. This sentence, like so many in the critical essays, derives its meaning from the relation between two or three or even four impressions, rather than from one central idea directly expressed.

This is not to say that some of the criticism does not come out more simply. There is always the sudden illumination produced by an unexpected analogy, as in an essay on Edith Sitwell:

In *Gold Coast Customs* I find for the first time in my contemporary reading a genius for invective as ferocious as Swift's (own), invective in the high-striding authoritative style, the same admirable stateliness of wrath, the savage indignation of a just mind and generous heart outraged to the far edge of endurance.[18]

or the sudden statement of a truth usually overlooked, the angle of vision adjusted to produce what quickly seems the right view, as in this contribution to the ever-lively controversy over Ezra Pound:

Pound was one of the most opiniated and unselfish men who ever lived, and he made friends and enemies everywhere by the simple exercise of the classic American constitutional right of free speech. His speech was free to outrageous license. He was completely reckless about making enemies. His so-called anti-Semitism was, hardly anyone has noted, only equalled by his anti-Christianism.[19]

Miss Porter's critical methods seem to operate least well, curiously enough, in an appraisal of Katherine Mansfield, written for *The Nation* in 1937. There is probably nothing seriously wrong with this piece, except that it never seems quite to give us what we expect: a fresh and vital view of a writer whose work lies so completely within Miss Porter's own domain. What we get, instead, is a fairly conventional view of the rare qualities in Katherine Mansfield's art which is lopped off rather suddenly by a notation on her personal tragedy. One is almost forced to conclude that Katherine Mansfield's art lies too close to Miss Porter's own, as the following would seem to indicate:

With fine objectivity she bares a moment of experience, real experience, in the life of some human being; she states no belief, gives no motives, airs no theories, but simply presents to the reader a situation, a place and a character, and there it is; and the emotional content is present as implicitly as the germ is in the grain of wheat.[20]

What could more accurately describe the method and effect of Miss Porter's own stories?

The second section of *The Days Before*, labelled by its author *Personal and Particular*, suffers from the limitations of this designation. It is at once the most and the least rewarding part of the book. It contains those remarkably clear statements of faith and belief from which I have already quoted, but it also contains much that is arbitrary and superficial. In this second category belong an arch and artificial attack on commercial writing, in which the tone quite overcomes the substance; the long essay on the rose and its water-colorist, Pierre-Joseph Redouté, which has some passages of rather showy verbal virtuosity and little else; some frankly trivial pieces like *A House of One's Own* and a descriptive excursion into the land of Audobon, which do not attempt to go beyond their set limits; and two pieces on marriage which annoy more frequently than they exalt, especially since Miss Porter seems in these to have deserted the hard real world of her fiction for the misty world of sentimentality. Balanced against all these, however, are the three statements on writing, the seven answers contributed to the *Partisan Review* symposium, and *Portrait: Old South*, a sketch of Miss Porter's past which must be read in conjuction with the Miranda stories to be appreciated. Miss Porter's answers to the questions submitted by the *Partisan Review* are concise and direct. She indicates, in addition to her preference for Henry James, that she has not been able to make a living by her writing, although she believes in literature as her profession; that she writes for no particular audience, although she believes that the audience for serious literature has been growing; that she suffers from the confusion of political tendencies (this was written in 1939) and tries to find her own way to a ground of personal belief; that she is a pacifist, and that she believes the responsibility of the artist to society "is the plain and simple responsibility of any other human being."[21] And she reiterates her purpose in her art:

My whole attempt has been to discover and understand human motives, human feelings, to make a distillation of what human relations and experiences my mind has been able to absorb. I have never known an uninteresting human being, and I have never known two alike; there are broad classifications and deep similarities, but I am interested in the thumbprint. I am passionately involved with these individuals who populate all these enormous migrations, calamities; these beings without which, one by one, all the "broad movements of history" could never take place. One by one—as they were born.[22]

There remains in the second section of *The Days Before* two pieces of importance in understanding Miss Porter, since they give evidence of what I have already called her sense of history. The first is called *American Statement: 4 July, 1942*, and, while it is not wholly free from sentimentality, represents a dedicated artist's determination to carry on in the face of whatever threats history may impose:

And during this period of suspension of the humanities, in the midst of the outrage and the world horror staggering to the imagination, we might find it profitable to examine the true nature of our threatened liberties, and their political, legal, and social origins and meanings, and decide exactly what their value is, and where we should be without them. They were not accidental by any means; they are implicit in our theory of government, which was in turn based on humanistic concepts of the importance of the individual and his rights in society. They are not mere ornaments on the facade, but are laid in the foundation stone of the structure, and they will last as long as the structure itself but no longer. They are not inalienable: the house was built with great labor and it is made with human hands; human hands can tear it down again, and will, if it is not well-loved and defended.[23]

The second piece is called *The Future Is Now*. It is a pointed statement on life in the atomic age, written for *Mademoiselle* in 1950. Miss Porter states the importance of the present moments as the means by which the future may be secured, and views the atomic bomb less as a dire threat than as a means of bringing us to our highest level of achievement, urged on by the odds of history:

And yet it may be that what we have is a world not on the verge of flying apart, but an uncreated one—still in shapeless fragments waiting to be put together properly. I imagine that when we want something better, we may have it: at perhaps no greater price than we have already paid for the worse.[24]

The third and concluding section of *The Days Before* is called simply *Mexican*, and it is the most fragmentary and least valuable part of the book. It opens with a long, effective critical and biographical essay on the Mexican author, Jose de Lizardi, an article which served originally as a preface to his book, *The Itching Parrot*, and which, by virtue of Miss Porter's lucid exposition of Mexico's and Lizardi's history, escapes being too highly specialized. But the rest is mostly inconclusive, consisting as it does of short pieces and sketches dating, often, from the formative years Miss Porter spent in Mexico. Perhaps the greatest value of the last section of *The Days Before* lies in the fact that it points the way towards stories like *Maria Concepcion*, the first story Miss Porter ever finished, *Flowering Judas* and *Hacienda*. The entire Mexican experience, in other words, speaks more eloquently in the fiction than it does in *The Days Before*. There is one other short piece of interest in these Mexican notes: a severe view of D. H. Lawrence's *The Plumed Serpent*, written when the novel first appeared in 1926. I do not think that it amounts to an accurate or impartial estimate of the book, but it throws light on Miss Porter, who judges Lawrence with an unexpected moral severity. She appreciates his "poetic force," at the same time that she is tired of his "despairs and futilities," his insistence on sex and the frustrations of a mechanized society. She laments the disappearance in abstract symbolism and shoddy mysticism of the former great artist:

When you have read this book read *Sons and Lovers* over again. You will realize the catastrophe that has overtaken Lawrence.[25]

And one somehow senses that Lawrence is perhaps the kind of writer to whom Miss Porter is naturally antipathetic: the writer enervated, rather than invigorated, by human society, doomed to hysteria and the facile shibboleth by the attrition of time and energy.

Taken altogether, then, *The Days Before* is an extraordinarily uneven book. Several of the pieces in it do not at all resemble the writer of the nevelettes and stories; but some others, and these are nearly always those dealing with the artist and the problems of his craft, represent Katherine Anne Porter working at the top of her powers.

But *The Days Before*, after all, operates only in the abstract, moving as it does among ideas, opinions, and impressions, sometimes rather injudiciously mixed. When we turn to the fiction, however, we are in the realm of established art, where there is not an adventitious sentence to distract us from the writer's shining purpose, and where every pointed word and polished phrase has an almost intolerably lucid relevance.

MIRANDA

The first six stories in *The Leaning Tower* deal with the childhood of Miranda, its magic atmosphere and the relatives who people it. All this is so skillfully, lovingly, tenderly evoked that one cannot escape wondering how much of it is based on Miss Porter's own memories of the South at the turn of the century and how much of it is purely imaginative.

These six stories, although nearly perfect in form, are not completely developed within themselves; each of them, and they vary in length from five pages to twenty-four, is a fragment, and it is only by piecing the six together that we get a connected picture of the people and the time. Miss Porter's method of communicating her material here is sometimes reminiscent of William Faulkner's in his Yoknapatawpha saga: frequently we are given information in one story that is of value to us only because of something we have learned in another. For instance, we are introduced, in *The Witness,* to Uncle Jimbilly, the manumitted slave, and then, in *The Old Order,* we meet Old Nannie, but not until we get to *The Last Leaf* do we learn that they have been married and are now living apart. Another reason why these six pieces are inevitably closer to the sketch than to the formal story is that they seem to aim at indication rather than narration. They present an intricately woven set of impressions, images, and details, out of which emerge the varied attributes of a personality. The emphasis, all through them, is on the character of the individual, and, most particularly, those elements in that character which contribute to its singularity. When events are described, or the past is revealed, it is only as a means of throwing new light on the individual.

Significantly enough, it is not Miranda who dominates the scene in these six stories. In only two of them does she appear as a central character; in one she is present only peripherally, and in the remaining three not at all. The central character is the Grandmother, who is presented to us in the first of the six stories, *The Source,*[26] preparing for her annual journey to her farm where she undertakes the vast business of setting it, and the households of its Negro tenants, in order; after which she returns to her town house, ready again "to set to work restoring to order the place which no doubt had gone somewhat astray in her absence." That she is the actual source of all stability in the world of her widower son and his three children (Miranda, Maria, and Paul) we have no doubt. The children "loved their Grandmother; she was the only reality to them in a world that seemed otherwise without fixed authority or refuge, since their mother had died so early that only the eldest girl remembered her vaguely: just the same they felt that Grandmother was tyrant, and they wished to be free of her; so they were always pleased when, on a certain day, as a sign that her visit was drawing to an end, she would go out to the pasture and call her old saddle-horse, Fiddler."

Fiddler, we learn in *The Old Order*,[27] represents the past, for that was the name of a pony the Grandmother had received from her father when she was a child, and "that name she reserved for a long series of saddle horses. She had named the first in honor of Fiddler Gay, an old Negro who made the music for dances and parties." And the old Grandmother herself represents the past, which, together with Old Nannie, her lifelong servant and friend, she remembers in the long Southern afternoons. "They talked about the past, really—always about the past. Even the future seemed like something gone and done with when they spoke of it. It did not seem an extension of their past, but a repetition of it." The Grandmother, fully aware of herself as the source of life and order, is given to saying, " 'I am the mother of eleven children,' " and " 'I have planted five orchards in three states, and now I see only one tree in bloom.' " She represents the order and stability of the past, qualities that neither her ineffectual son, Harry, nor any of his three children, is equipped to carry forward.

Harry and his children had lived under a "matriarchal tyranny," but when it passed there was no system of life to replace it. The Grandmother died suddenly, in the spirit in which she had lived; she "came into the house quite flushed and exhilarated, saying how well she felt in the bracing mountain air—and dropped dead over the doorsill." She had been "the great-granddaughter of Kentucky's most famous pioneer," and "the daughter of a notably heroic captain in the War of 1812." She had kept the splendor of the past before her grandchildren, the same past to which Nannie rendered mute testimony, and, after her death, we learn in the story entitled *The Grave*,[28] "It was said the motherless family was running down, with the Grandmother no longer there to hold it together."

In *The Old Order*, the longest piece of the six, Miss Porter gives us a record of the Grandmother's life, and here we can see how little conventional narrative devices are to her point; the Grandmother's life is recapitulated by details related in a complex method of moving backwards and forwards in time. The piece opens with the Grandmother and Nannie sitting down to one of their reminiscent afternoons, goes back to the Grandmother's childhood and the time of Nannie's coming to the family as the child of two newly-purchased slaves, and continues to come forward and go backward as the points of the Grandmother's characterization dictate, until, at the end, it leaps suddenly ahead to

17

her death. Miss Sophia Jane, we learn, had been "married off" when she was seventeen "in a very gay wedding," in Kentucky. Then, long after she was married, she saw in her husband "all the faults she had most abhorred in her elder brother: lack of aim, failure to act at crises, a philosophic detachment from practical affairs, a tendency to set projects on foot and then leave them to perish or to be finished by some- one else; and a profound conviction that everyone around him should be happy to wait upon him hand and foot." Meanwhile, "the Grandmother developed a character truly portentous under the discipline of trying to change the characters of others," and her husband "disliked and feared her deadly wilfullness, her certainty that her ways were not only right but beyond criticism, that her feelings were important, even in the lightest matter, and must not be tampered with or treated casually."

But "not until she was in middle age, her husband dead, her property dispersed, and she found herself with a houseful of children, making a new life for them in another place, with all the responsibilities of a man but none of the privileges, did she finally emerge into something like an honest life: and yet, she was passionately honest. She had never been anything else." She had come to despise men, we are told, but she was ruled by them. "Her husband threw away her dowry and her property in wild investments in strange territories: Louisiana, Texas; and without protest she watched him play her substance like a gambler." Then he "had fought stubbornly through the War . . . had been wound- ed, had lingered helpless, and had died of his wound long after the great fever and excitement had faded in hopeless defeat, when to be a man ruined and wounded in the War was merely to have proved oneself, perhaps, more heroic than wise." So the Grandmother took her family and set out for Louisiana where her husband had purchased a sugar refinery, but she "had hardly repaired the house she bought and got the orchard planted when she saw that, in her hands, the sugar refinery was going to be a failure." And on she went to an unsettled part of Texas with her nine children (two had died) and seven Negroes. All the while she mourned her husband "with dry eyes, angrily." And finally, twenty years later, she recognized his features in a grandchild, "and wept."

During the second year in Texas, "two of her younger sons, Harry and Robert, suddenly ran away." When they had been returned by a neighbor, their mother found "that they had wanted to go back to Louisiana to eat sugar cane. They had been thinking about sugar cane all winter . . . their mother was stunned. She had built a house large enough to shelter them all, of hand-sawed lumber dragged by ox-cart for forty miles, she had got the fields fenced in and the crops planted, she had, she believed, fed and clothed her children; and now she realized they were hungry . . . Sitting there with her arms around them, she felt her heart break in her breast. She had thought it was a silly phrase. It happened to her. It was not that she was incapable of feeling afterward, for in a way she was more emotional, more quick, but griefs never again lasted with her so long as they had before. This day was the beginning of her spoiling her children and being afraid of them." When they began to marry, "she was able to give them each a good strip of land and a little money . . . and she saw them all begin well, though not all of them ended so." Then, when Harry's wife, of whom she never approved, died, "the Grandmother took the children and began life again, with almost the same zest, and with more indulgence . . . She had just got them brought up to the point where she felt she could begin to work the faults out of them—faults inherited, she admitted freely, from both sides of the house—when she died." She had been visiting a son and daughter-in-law in West Texas, interfering in and ruling over their household even to the extent of "moving a fifty-foot adobe wall," when she "dropped dead over the doorsill."

When the Grandmother and Nannie had sat and talked about the past, they had discussed "religion, and the slack way the world was going nowadays, and . . . the younger children, whom these topics always brought to mind." Nannie deplored Maria and Paul and Miranda as "new-fangled grandchildren," and both she and the Grandmother had settled ideas about children and their upbringing. "Childhood was a long state of instruction and probation for adult life, which was in turn a long, severe, undeviating devotion to duty, the largest part of which consisted in bringing up children." A firm and hardy stock was thus preserved from generation to generation, but when the controlling forces, like the Grandmother and Nannie, died or went away, the stock was in danger of thinning out. In these six sketches of the atmosphere of Miranda's childhood, we sense quite plainly that all the family greatness seems to lie in the past, with the Grandmother and her memories.

In the two pieces in which Miranda herself appears directly, the uncertain future, dark and frightening, looms in front of her. In *The Circus*,[29] the small Miranda is frightened by a clown performing acrobatics on a wire, and the colored servant, Dicey, removes her from the circus tent at the Grandmother's command. On the way out, Miranda encounters a dwarf. "Miranda almost touched him before she saw him, her distorted face with its open mouth and glistening tears almost level with his. He leaned forward and peered at her with kind, not-human golden eyes, like a near-sighted dog: then made a horrid grimace at her, imitating her own face. Miranda struck at him in sheer ill-temper, screaming. Dicey drew her away quickly, but not before Miranda had seen in his face, suddenly, a look of haughty, remote displeasure, a true grown-up look. She knew it well. It chilled her with a new kind of fear: she had not believed he was really human."

In *The Grave*, the mysterious adult world reveals itself again, when

Miranda's brother Paul shoots a rabbit and exposes the litter it had been about to bear. Miranda "looked and looked—excited, but not frightened, for she was accustomed to the sight of animals killed in hunting—filled with pity and astonishment and a kind of shocked delight in the wonderful little creatures for their own sakes, they were so pretty. 'Ah, there's blood running over them,' she said and began to tremble without knowing why. Yet she wanted most deeply to see and to know. Having seen, she felt at once as if she had known all along." And she loses her experience in the vast abyss of memory, only to recall it twenty years later, walking through a market in a strange city.

Though the Miranda who appears in these sketches is still only a young child (in *The Grave*, the last of the six pieces, she is nine years old), she is very much aware of the complex, baffling world of adults and of the isolated experiences which point towards the knowledge of adults. Meanwhile she lives with her father or her brother and sister in the town house or the country house or on the farm. And while the Grandmother and Nannie are present, she is safe. But they must inevitably disappear.

In the last two of these six sketches, the Grandmother is dead, and her loss is felt as keenly as her presence had been. She was indeed "the source," just as she had represented "authority." She imposed her own order and design on the world. She was the last of the waning pioneer stock, and she had been full of courage because she had known the failure of love and hope. What she most represented, of course, was strength and fortitude (very high values in Miss Porter's scales, as we shall see), but these she passed on to one of her grandchildren. Miranda, too, is a moral aristocrat, and her life, different as it is to be from her Grandmother's, reveals how much of the older woman's training and personality the small child absorbed.

When we turn to two of the three novelettes that make up Miss Porter's second book, *Pale Horse, Pale Rider*, we get the story of Miranda herself. The first of these, *Old Mortality*,[30] is a miracle of compression; in approximately 20,000 words, Miss Porter tells us all we need to know about Miranda's childhood, and the legends from the past which shaped it; then she goes on to show us, quite dramatically, how these legends inevitably affect Miranda as she comes to maturity. *Old Mortality* falls into three sections marked out by the author; the first is dated 1885-1902, the second, 1904, and the third, 1912.

In the first part of *Old Mortality*, the Grandmother is still alive, and representing, as always, the past. She is the guardian of its history and the keeper of its relics. "Photographs, portraits by inept painters who meant earnestly to flatter, and the festival garments folded away in dried herbs and camphor were disappointing when the little girls tried to fit them to the living beings created in their minds by the breathing words of their elders."

The past, splendidly romantic and always redolent of a promise that the present never seems to fulfill, is dramatically projected in the figure of Miranda's and Maria's Aunt Amy, who died when she was still very young. Her portrait hangs in the living-room and draws the little girls' eyes again and again. Her beauty is recognized by all her relatives as being superior to that of any other member of the family. The children are forever clamoring to be told this or that fragment of her story, and some relative is always ready to oblige; so that, piece by piece, her sad, romantic history unfolds in their minds.

Amy had been doomed to early death by tuberculosis, but her disease had not kept her from being the belle of every ball she attended, or from tormenting the man she was eventually to marry. "Uncle Gabriel had waited five years to marry Aunt Amy. She had been ill, her chest was weak; she was engaged twice to other young men and broke her engagements for no reason; and she laughed at the advice of older and kinder-hearted persons who thought it very capricious of her not to return the devotion of such a handsome and romantic young man as Gabriel, her second cousin, too; it was not as if she would be marrying a stranger."

But Amy persisted in her mistreatment of Gabriel, and then the scandal broke; she flirted at a masked ball with her former suitor, Raymond, and was even thought to have kissed him; an indiscretion which provoked her brother, Harry, the children's father, into shooting at the man before Gabriel could challenge him to a duel. This was the ball for which "Amy copied her costume from a small Dresden-china shepherdess which stood on the mantelpiece in the parlor."

The morning after the ball, Harry, accompanied by his brother, Bill, and Gabriel, struck out for Mexico to wait until the scandal would blow over. Amy woke early, in a fever, and set out after them; she "rode to the border, kissed her brother Harry good-by, and rode back again with Bill and Gabriel." Then she sent Gabriel away, and took to her bed; but, later, following a hemorrhage, she asked for him. When he appeared, he had just been disinherited by his grandfather who disapproved of his devotion to horses and racetracks. But, finally, Amy agreed to marry him, saying, " 'Gabriel, if we get married now there'll be just time to be in New Orleans for Mardi Gras.' " So she was married, and off they went. " 'She ran into the gray cold and stepped into the carriage and turned and smiled with her face as pale as death,' " Miranda and Maria are often told, " 'and called out, 'Goodby, good-by,' and refused her cloak, and said, 'Give me a glass of wine.' And none of us ever saw her alive again.' " For, just six weeks later, Amy was dead in New Orleans.

Now, in the year 1902, the little girls are surrounded by Amy's story, played out seventeen years in the past. There are still some family splendors, like cousin Isabel. "When Cousin Isabel came out in her

tight black riding habit, surrounded by young men, and mounted grace-
fully. . . . Miranda's heart would close with such a keen dart of admira-
tion, envy, vicarious pride it was almost painful." On the other hand,
there is Cousin Eva, "shy and chinless, straining her upper lip over two
enormous teeth, (sitting) in corners watching her mother. . . . She wore
her mother's old clothes, made over, and taught Latin in a Female Seminary. She believed in votes for women, and had travelled about, making speeches." Miranda, naturally enough, identifies herself with the
romantic side of her family, and "persisted through her childhood in
believing, in spite of her smallness, thinness, her little snubby nose
saddled with freckles, her speckled gray eyes and habitual tantrums,
that by some miracle she would grow into a tall, cream-colored bru-
nette, like cousin Isabel; she decided always to wear a trailing white
satin gown."

Meanwhile, the past asserts itself ever more strongly. "Grandmother
in her youth had heard Jenny Lind, and thought that Nellie Melba was
much overrated. Father had seen Bernhardt, and Madame Modjeska
was no sort of rival." At the same time, Miranda wonders about Aunt
Amy, looks at her old-fashioned portrait, and listens to the stories of
her life. Miranda has never seen her Uncle Gabriel, however, since he
has remarried and lives in New Orleans. But she continues to think of
his love for Amy as "such a story as one found in old books: unworldly
books, but true, such as the Vita Nuova, the Sonnets of Shakespeare,
and the Wedding Song of Spenser; and poems by Edgar Allan Poe."
And Miranda also knows the poem he had written for Amy's gravestone:

> " 'She lives again who suffered life,
>   Then suffered death, and now set free
>   A singing angel, she forgets
>   The griefs of old mortality.' "

The meaning of the second part of *Old Mortality* is quite clear: the
cracks are beginning to appear in the legend of the past. The year is
1904, and Maria and Miranda are attending a convent school in New
Orleans, in which "they referred to themselves as 'immured.' It gave a
romantic glint to what was otherwise a very dull life for them, except
for blessed Saturday afternoons during the racing season." On these
Saturdays, their father or another relative usually appeared to take
them for an outing, often to the racetracks. Miranda, watching the
horses circling the track, longed to be a jockey when she grew up, and
determined to practice her riding. On one particular Saturday, however, her father takes her and Maria to a track where one of the horses
in the running is owned by their Uncle Gabriel, whom they still know
only by the role he had played in Aunt Amy's legend. The horse is a
hundred to one shot, which "Miranda knew well enough . . . . was no
bet at all." But she is distracted from thinking of her bet by her first

sight of Uncle Gabriel, who hails the girls and their father from a lower level of the grandstand. "He was a shabby fat man with bloodshot blue eyes, sad beaten eyes, and a big melancholy laugh, like a groan." He looks at his two nieces, and says to Harry, "'Pretty as pictures, but rolled into one they don't come up to Amy, do they?'" The appearance of their uncle disturbs the girls, and they miss most of the race, until their father warns them, "'Watch Miss Lucy come home.'" and they rise in their seats to see Uncle Gabriel's horse streak past the judge's stand. The girls have each won a hundred dollars, but their triumph is hollow in the face of their disillusionment with their uncle, who insists on taking them and their father to visit his second wife. And now the girls, "watching Uncle Gabriel's lumbering, unsteady back, were thinking that this was the first time they had ever seen a man that they knew to be drunk. . . . Miranda felt it was an important moment in a great many ways."

The failure of the great legend becomes complete when Harry and his daughters meet Honey, Gabriel's second wife, and Gabriel's demoralization is apparent. The uncle and his wife are living in a dingy, third-rate hotel lost in the back areas of New Orleans, beyond the Negro quarter. Honey shows no joy at all in the arrival of her husband's nieces, for she is beyond all joy. Gabriel informs her that his horse has won, and says, "'We'll move to the St. Charles tomorrow. Get your best dresses together, Honey, the long dry spell is over.'" But Honey knows better: "'I've lived in the St. Charles before, and I've lived here before,' she said, in a tight deliberate voice, 'and this time I'll just stay where I am, thank you. I prefer it to moving back here in three months. I'm settled now, I feel at home here.'" Maria and Miranda "sat trying not to stare, miserably ill at ease," until finally their father rises to leave. The girls cannot wait to be gone, and in the taxi on the way back to school, "Miranda sat thinking so hard she forgot and spoke out in her thoughtless way: 'I've decided I'm not going to be a jockey after all.'"

If in this second part of *Old Mortality*, the legend fails Miranda, in the third and final section she breaks with it, and her voluminous, echoing past, which extends back so far beyond her birth, dramatically but inevitably. And now we see the logical conclusion for which Miss Porter, all the while, has been preparing us. The time is 1912, and Miranda is now eighteen; we find out that she has eloped from school the year before, and married, and, when we meet her, she is on the train, coming home for Uncle Gabriel's funeral. Here she encounters an old lady who has "two immense front teeth and a receding chin," but who does not "lack character," and who turns out to be Cousin Eva, the feminist, who had symbolized, in Miranda's childhood, the ugliness of the family. The two women naturally fall to talking of the past and of their relatives, for Eva has been away a long time. Once, Miranda looks at her with a "painful premonition," and thinks, "'Oh, must I ever be like that?'" Eva has lost her chair at the Seminary and has been to jail three times in her struggle for the Women's Vote.

When the conversation turns to Aunt Amy, Eva airs her opinion. "'Your Aunt Amy was a devil and a mischief-maker, but I loved her dearly. I used to stand up for Amy when her reputation wasn't worth that,'" and Eva's "fingers snapped like castanets." Later she says, "'She went through life like a spoiled darling, doing as she pleased and letting other people suffer for it, and pick up the pieces after her.'" And, as she keeps thinking of Amy, Eva's views become increasingly severe: "'The way she rose up suddenly from death's door to marry Gabriel Breaux, after refusing him and treating him like a dog for years, looked odd, to say the least.... And there was something very mysterious about her death, only six weeks after marriage.'" Finally, Eva says: "'What I ask myself, what I ask myself over and over again,' she whispered, 'is, what connection did this man Raymond .... have with Amy's sudden marriage to Gabriel, and *what* did Amy do to make away with herself so soon afterward? For mark my words, child, Amy wasn't so ill as all that. She'd been flying around for years after the doctors said her lungs were weak. Amy did away with herself to escape some disgrace, some exposure that she faced.'" Eva continues, talking of all the girls of Amy's time, their dances and their rivalries, from both of which Eva herself was shut out. Finally, "'It was just sex,' she said in despair; 'their minds dwelt on nothing else. They didn't call it that, it was all smothered under pretty names, but that's all it was, sex.'"

When Eva thinks of herself, she becomes all the more bitter towards her family. "'All my life the whole family bedevilled me about my chin. My entire girlhood was spoiled by it. Can you imagine,' she asked, with a ferocity that seemed much too deep for this one cause, 'people who call themselves civilized spoiling life for a young girl because she had one unlucky feature.... Ah, the family' she said, releasing her breath and sitting back quietly, 'the whole hideous institution should be wiped from the face of the earth. It is the root of all human wrongs,' she ended, and relaxed, and her face became calm."

Miranda listens to all of this, and Cousin Eva says finally, "'I wanted you to hear the other side of the story.'" Then Miranda retires for the night, and falls instantly asleep. In the morning, her father is on the platform, waiting for her, and he and Eva begin to lament Gabriel. Miranda, sitting with the Negro boy in the car that is taking her to her old home, hears her father and Eva chattering on in the rear. They are talking about the only subject they can ever discuss: family history. And suddenly, with sure, firm strokes, Miss Porter concludes her story with what I believe is one of the most eloquent, direct and meaningful passages in our contemporary prose. Miranda realizes abruptly how sick she is of these same old narratives, how smothered she has been by her family, grandparents, aunts, uncles, and cousins, how little she shares their interminable interest in the past. She determines in her mind to leave her old home once and for all, and not to return to marriage:

"She would have no more bonds that smothered her in love and hatred. She knew now why she had run away to marriage, and she knew that she was going to run away from marriage, and she was not going to stay in any place, with anyone, that threatened to forbid her making her own discoveries, that said "No" to her. . . . Oh, what is life, she asked herself in desperate seriousness, in those childish unanswerable words, and what shall I do with it? It is something of my own, she thought in a fury of jealous possessiveness, what shall I make of it? . . . What is the truth, she asked herself as intently as if the question had never been asked, the truth, even about the smallest, the least important of all the things I must find out? and where shall I begin to look for it? Her mind closed stubbornly against remembering, not the past but the legend of the past, other people's memory of the past. . . . Ah, but there is my own life to come yet, she thought, my own life now and beyond. I don't want any promises, I won't have any false hopes, I won't be romantic about myself. I can't live in their world any longer, she told herself, listening to the voices back of her. Let them tell their stories to each other. Let them go on explaining how things happened. I don't care. At least I can know the truth about what happens to me, she assured herself silently, making a promise to herself, in her hopefullness, her ignorance."[31]

And this magnificent forward-leap of Miranda's mind seems somehow to encompass all her previous history.

When we turn to the second Miranda novelette, *Pale Horse, Pale Rider*, we can see the significance of the stress on "her ignorance" which concludes *Old Mortality*. In this second story, the year is 1918, the last of the war, and Miranda is no longer as ignorant or as naive as she was when she promised herself independence in 1912. *Pale Horse, Pale Rider* is more a mood piece and less a sustained narrative than *Old Mortality*; its action is confined to a brief, haunted period and its stage is carefully set for doom by a skillful use of symbols and details. In one sense at least, *Pale Horse, Pale Rider* is, as its title implies, a story of presentiment, a concrete embodiment of what I have called Miss Porter's sense of disaster. The disaster here is represented by the huge public forces, war and disease, which invade and destroy the private right to happiness.

The plot is very simple. Miranda is working on a newspaper in a Southwestern city, near which there is a large army camp. Before the story opens, she has met a soldier of her own age, Adam, and has begun to fall in love with him. She loves him almost against her will, however, since she believes that real love, in such a time and place, can have no happy outcome. The influenza epidemic has begun to rage throughout the country. On the morning on which the story commences, Miranda awakes from a dream of doom and rises, feeling an unaccountable malaise. She bathes, dresses, and waits for Adam, thinking meanwhile of two men who had come to her office the day before to try to pressure her into buying a Liberty Bond she can not possibly afford. Adam arrives, and walks with her to the office. There she chats with her co-workers, Chuck and Towney, confronts a third-rate vaudeville performer who comes in to upbraid her for having written an unfavorable review of his show, and takes Chuck off to another show for which she must write another review. She is beginning by this time to feel ill, though she does not admit this to herself. After the show, she meets Adam, whom she takes to still another play. Adam waits in a restaurant while she writes her review and they go off together to dance. The next day, Miranda is terribly ill, able only to phone Bill, another of her colleagues on the newspaper, who is attempting to get her a doctor and a hospital bed. Meanwhile Adam arrives with coffee and medicine and watches over her and even talks to her in between her bouts of delirium. When he goes out to replenish the supply of coffee, some doctors appear and remove Miranda to a hospital. In the hospital she receives a note from Adam, saying that he had returned to find her gone, and that he has been refused admission to the hospital. There follows a prolonged illness for Miranda, an illness in which she meets and recognizes death but only to return to life. Strangely, however, she finds life less desirable than she had before her illness. She feels wan, disillusioned, almost old. On the day that Chuck and Towney appear to take her home, she opens a letter from a man in Adam's camp informing her that Adam has died during her illness.

That is really all there is to the plot. What makes *Pale Horse, Pale Rider* such a moving and unforgettable work of art is the nearly incredible precision of its language particularly in those parts which describe Miranda's confrontation of death, and the haunted atmosphere which Miss Porter evokes in telling her story. Like all art of the first order, it leaves us with the impression of having shared in an actual experience, rather than merely having read about it.

The atmosphere is sustained by an adroit and unobtrusive use of symbols and details which have an immediate effect on us even before we can recognize their meanings. In her dream, at the beginning of the story, Miranda is back in the house of her childhood, and her thoughts echo *Old Mortality*:

How I have loved this house in the morning before we are all awake and tangled together like badly cast fishing lines. Too many people have been born here, and have wept too much here, and have laughed too much, and have been too angry and outrageous with each other here. Too many have died in this bed already, there are far too many ancestral bones propped up on the mantelpieces, there have been too damned many anti-macassars in this house, she said loudly, and oh, what accumulation of storied dust never allowed to settle in peace for one moment.[32]

And, just as the unobtrusive but persuasive reiteration of the word "too" gives to this passage its particular rhythm and cumulative meaning, so the symbols and details of *Pale Horse, Pale Rider* underline and prepare us for its tragic impact. In the dream, Miranda rides out on the old family horse, Graylie (after deciding not to take Fiddler), and a pale, greenish stranger rides after her. Taking Graylie's bridle, Miranda tells the horse that they must outrun "Death and the Devil." But the stranger rides with her:

The stranger rode beside her, easily, lightly, his reins loose in his half-closed hand, straight and elegant in dark shabby garments that flapped upon his bones; his pale face smiled in an evil trance, he did not glance at her. Ah, I have seen this fellow before, I know this man if I could place him. He is no stranger to me.

She pulled Graylie up, rose in her stirrups and shouted, I'm not going with you this time—ride on! Without pausing or turning his head the stranger rode on.[33]

Excepting Miranda's growing love for Adam, this dream gives us the whole of what is to come. And the mood created by the dream is sustained in the details of everyday living under the shadow of war and disease: the seedy, shabby men who had come to Miranda about buying a Liberty Bond had somehow seemed to threaten her, telling her "it wasn't so much her fifty dollars that was going to make any difference. It was just a pledge of good faith on her part. A pledge of good faith that she was a loyal American doing her duty," and they had stopped at the head of the stairs on their way out, "lighting cigars and wedging their hats more firmly over their eyes"; Towney, the Society Editor, had been discovered in the cloakroom by Miranda, where she was "quietly hysterical" because the men had told her she would lose her job if she didn't buy a bond; and Miranda had spent the whole day among society women "wallowing in good works.... setting out, a gay procession of high-powered cars and brightly tinted faces to cheer the brave boys who already, you might very well say, had fallen in defense of their country."

But this particular day is to be no better. Miranda, walking with Adam towards her office, passes first one funeral procession and then another:

"It seems to be a plague," said Miranda, "something out of the Middle Ages. Did you ever see so many funerals, ever?"

"Never did. Well, let's be strong minded and not have any of it. I've got four days straight from the blue and not a blade of grass must grow under our feet. What about tonight?"[34]

And, in the drugstore, having breakfast with Adam, Miranda realizes she could love Adam:

She liked him, she liked him, and there was more than this but it was no good even imagining, because he was not for her nor for any woman, being beyond experience already, committed without any knowledge or act of his own to death.[35]

Later, leaving the theater with Chuck, the sportswriter, Miranda watches the crowds in the aisles moving towards the exits:

What did I ever know about them? There must be a great many of them here who think as I do, and we dare not say a word to each other of our desperation, we are speechless animals letting ourselves be destroyed, and why? Does anybody here believe the things we say to each other?[36]

Later that evening, after Miranda has written her review, she comes out to the street and goes towards the restaurant where Adam is waiting for her. She is feeling quite ill by now, and when she sees Adam's face by the window of the restaurant, she has the most terrible of her premonitions:

It was an extraordinary face, smooth and fine and golden in the shabby light, but now set in a blind melancholy, a look of pained suspense and disillusion. For just one split second she got a glimpse of Adam when he would have been older, the face of the man he would not live to be.[37]

While Adam and Miranda are dancing, Miranda notices a woman at a table weeping and being consoled by her man, who holds and kisses her hand. Miranda envies them:

It was enviable, enviable, that they could sit quietly together and have the same expression on their faces while they looked into the hell they shared, no matter what kind of hell, it was theirs, they were together.[38]

Suddenly we leap forward into the twilight world of Miranda's illness, into what may be called the second part of *Pale Horse, Pale Rider*. For the next day, she is very ill, and the landscapes of her mind are different from those of reality. And it is here, I believe, that Miss Porter reaches the deepest and most meaningful level of her art. The imagination and lucidity which she brings to her description of Miranda's illness seem to me to make *Pale Horse, Pale Rider* the height of her achievement. Though she reveals these qualities constantly, of course, in her fiction, nowhere else is the human situation quite so deeply felt and purely conveyed. And nowhere else is the final irony quite so tragic.

While Adam has gone out to have a prescription filled, Miranda lies in bed, thinking:

I suppose I should ask to be sent home, she thought, it's a respectable old custom to inflict your death on the family if you can manage it. No, I'll stay here, this is my business, but not in this room, I hope.... I wish I were in the cold mountains in the snow, that's what I should like best; and all about her rose the measured ranges of the Rockies wearing their perpetual snow, their majestic blue laurels of cloud, chilling her to the bone with their sharp breath. Oh, no, I must have warmth —and her memory turned and roved after another place she had known first and loved best, that now she could see only in drifting fragments of palm and cedar, dark shadows and a sky that warmed without dazzling, as this strange sky had dazzled without warming her.[39]

Miss Porter's method of rendering Miranda's illness shows clearly in this passage. She uses a kind of stream of consciousness, introducing us directly to Miranda's thoughts ("Oh, no, I must have warmth,"), and then goes on to give us her own evocation of the scenes Miranda's imagination conjures up. This mixture of a direct transcription of Miranda's thoughts with Miss Porter's own more literal description of the embodiments of those thoughts is used throughout *Pale Horse, Pale Rider*. We have, therefore, two kinds of methods interwoven to carry us forward, the mental image, seen or longed for, reinforced by the description of its physical attributes. The story proceeds in the same way in the delirious moments of illness, when the images of fantasy and those of reality are merged in Miranda's mind.

Miranda imagines herself in

a writhing terribly alive and secret place of death, creeping with tangles of spotted serpents, rainbow-colored birds with malign eyes, leopards with humanly wise faces and extravagantly crested lions; screaming long-armed monkeys tumbling among broad fleshy leaves that glowed with sulpur-colored light and exuded the ichor of death, and rotting trunks of unfamiliar trees sprawled in crawling slime.

and she hears

two words only rising and falling and clamoring about her head. Danger, danger, danger, the voices said, and War, war, war.[40]

From these weird subjective states, made up of the prodigal images which the imagination of desperate illness sees and of the cold threats of the words which it hears, we are suddenly brought back to the plane of reality; Adam reenters Miranda's room and commences an argument with her landlady, who wishes to remove her tenant from the house immediately. This Miranda overhears, and says to Adam:

"It's a nice prospect, isn't it?"

"I've got your medicine," said Adam, "and you're to begin with it this minute. She can't put you out."

"So it's really as bad as that," said Miranda.

"It's as bad as anything can be," said Adam, "all the theaters and nearly all the shops and restaurants are closed, and the streets have been full of funerals all day and ambulances all night—"

"But not for me," said Miranda, feeling hilarious and lightheaded.[41]

Miranda suddenly sees her life threatened by death. She determines to live at the same time that she is afraid she is going to die:

"You'd get the notion I had a very sad life," she said, "and perhaps it was, but I'd be glad enough to have it now. If I could have it back, it would be easy to be happy about almost anything at all. That's not true, but that's the way I feel now." After a pause, she said, "There's nothing to tell if it ends now, for all this time I was getting ready for something that was going to happen later, when the time came. So now it's nothing much."[42]

A moment later, she asks Adam:

"Don't you love being alive? Don't you love weather and the colors at different times of the day, all the sounds and noises like children screaming in the next lot, and automobile horns and little bands playing in the street and the smell of food cooking?"

"I love to swim, too," said Adam.

"So do I," said Miranda; "we never did swim together."[43]

Then she and Adam begin to sing, "Pale horse, pale rider, done take my lover away."

"There's a lot more to it than that," said Adam, "about forty verses, the rider done taken away mammy, pappy, brother, sister, the whole family besides the lover—"

"But not the singer, not yet," said Miranda. "Death always leaves one singer to mourn. Death," she sang, "oh, leave one singer to mourn—"[44]

Suddenly she lies back on her pillows and thinks:

I must give up, I can't hold out any longer. There was only that pain, only that room, and only Adam. There were no longer any multiple planes of living, no tough filaments of memory and hope pulling taut backwards and forwards holding her upright between them. There was only this one moment and it was a dream of time, and Adam's face, very near hers, eyes still and intent, was a shadow, and there was to be nothing more...[45]

Then, "almost with no warning at all, she floated into the darkness, holding his hand, in sleep that was not sleep but clear evening light in a small green wood," and here, as if she realizes that these few scant scenes of her illness are to represent the culmination of her and Adam's love, as if she knows that doom has caught up with them and that her lover has met the sacrifice for which he has been marked out, she has a vision of arrows flying in which Adam finally lies dead, but she remains unwounded, untouched. Finally she screams, and Adam runs to her; but Miranda has seen his fate, has recognized the risk he runs in staying with her in her illness, a testament to his love for her.

Later, in the hospital, after Miss Tanner, the nurse, has read her Adam's note, Miranda has her final confrontation with death:

There it is, there it is at last, it is very simple; and soft carefully shaped words like oblivion and eternity are curtains hung before nothing at all. I shall not know when it happens, I shall not feel or remember, why can't I consent now, I am lost, there is no hope for me. Look, she told herself, there it is, that is death and there is nothing to fear. But she could not consent, still shrinking stiffly against the granite wall that was her childhood dream of safety, breathing slowly for fear of squandering breath, saying desperately, Look, don't be afraid, it is nothing, it is only eternity.

Granite walls, whirlpools, stars are things. None of them is death, nor the image of it. Death is death, said Miranda, and for the dead it has no attributes. Silenced she sank easily through deeps under deeps of darkness until she lay like a stone at the farthest bottom of life, knowing herself to be blind, deaf, speechless, no longer aware of the members of her own body, entirely withdrawn from all human concerns, yet alive with a peculiar lucidity and coherence; all notions of the mind, the reasonable inquiries of doubt, all ties of blood and the desires of the heart, dissolved and fell away from her, and there remained of her only a minute fiercely burning particle of being that knew itself alone, that relied upon nothing beyond itself for its strength; not susceptible to any appeal or inducement, being itself composed entirely of one single motive, the stubborn will to live. This fiery motionless particle set itself unaided to resist destruction, to survive and be in its own madness of being, motiveless and planless beyond that one essential end. Trust me, the hard unwinking angry point of light said. Trust me. I stay.[46]

And Miranda follows the point of light to a "deep clear landscape of sea and sand, of soft meadow and sky, freshly washed and glistening with transparencies of blue," and comes away from death and slowly back to life, wondering, "Where are the dead? We have forgotten the dead, oh, the dead, where are they?"

Coming to life again, Miranda hears bells, horns, and whistles mingling, and discovers that this "far clamor" is the armistice, the end of war but not of life.

And only now she discovers that she does not want life. She tries to reassure herself:

That was a child's dream of the heavenly meadow, the vision of repose that comes to a tired body in sleep, she thought, but I have seen it when I did not know it was a dream. Closing her eyes she would rest for a moment remembering that bliss which had repaid all the pain of the journey to reach it; opening them again she saw with a new anguish the dull world to which she was condemned, where the light seemed filmed over with cobwebs, all the bright surfaces corroded, the sharp planes melted and formless, all objects and beings meaningless, ah, dead and withered things that believed themselves alive.[47]

She has earned her way to heroism, fought the greatest adversary of all, and now the substance of life itself seems disappointing, and at night she wept "silently, shamelessly, in pity for herself and her lost rapture," longed for the great lighted visions of her most heroic moment.

But her greatest tragedy, her final disillusionment, the last gratuitous sacrifice is yet to come. When Chuck and Towney come to take her home, to secure the things she wants to begin her life again, Miranda opens the pile of letters that have accumulated during her illness. Only now does she realize how long she has been ill, for time itself has been a blur of delirium and semi-consciousness. "What a victory, what triumph, what happiness to be alive, sang the letters in a chorus." Happiness? One of the letters "was from a strange man at the camp where Adam had been, telling her that Adam had died of influenza in the camp hospital." So he had sufficiently taken her disease unto himself, and all Miranda's visions of doom are now fulfilled.

Miranda does not say a word about this letter, but goes on enumerating for Towney and Chuck the trivial things she needs. And when they go, she realizes that the time has come for her to leave the hospital, to begin saying good-by to her nurse and her doctor. Then, alone in her room:

Adam, she said, now you need not die again, but still I wish you were here; I wish you had come back, what do you think I came back for, Adam, to be deceived like this?

At once he was there beside her, invisibly but urgently present, a ghost but more alive than she was, the last intolerable cheat of her heart; for knowing it was false she still clung to the lie, the unpardonable lie of her bitter desire. She said, "I love you," and stood up trembling, trying by the mere act of her will to bring him to sight before her. If I could call you up from the grave I would, she said, if I could see your ghost I would say I believe. . . . "I believe," she said aloud, "Oh, let me see you once more."[48]

At this moment, perhaps, Miranda comes full circle and meets her grandmother, whose heart had broken in two when she knew her sons were hungry. Now, at last, she is more than ever the granddaughter of the ancestor whose own children she had rejected, and whose strength now passes on to her. Miranda, too, will lead a joyless life, threatened and insecure, armed only with her fortitude to face the emptiness of a life to which she has heroically regained her right. And so she goes again into the world, another Miranda altogether from the one she had been in the past; with the mark of tragedy in her heart, she turns again to the vagueness and sorrow conveyed in the final, ironic lines of *Pale Horse, Pale Rider*:

No more war, no more plague, only the dazed silence that follows the ceasing of the heavy guns; noiseless houses with the shades drawn, empty streets, the dead cold light of tomorrow. Now there would be time for everything.[49]

How far Miranda's chronical is composed of Miss Porter's personal history cannot be absolutely determined. But when we turn to *The Days Before*, to a tenderly written little memoir called *Portrait: Old South*, we come across such an obvious parallel as this:

I am the grandchild of a lost War, and I have blood-knowledge of what life can be in a defeated country on the bare bones of privation. The older people in my family used to tell such amusing little stories about it. One time, several years after the War ended, two small brothers (one of them was my father) set out by themselves on foot from their new home in south Texas, and when neighbors picked them up three miles from home, hundreds of miles from their goal, and asked them where they thought they were going, they answered confidently, "To Louisiana, to eat sugar cane," for they hadn't tasted sugar for months and remembered the happy times in my grandmother's cane fields there.[50]

We are given also a short history of Miss Porter's own grandmother,[51] who was married "in a Kentucky wedding somewhere around 1850," and for whom "the evil turn of fortune in her life tapped the bottomless reserves of her character, and her life was truly heroic. . . . The long difficulties of her life she regarded as temporary, an unnatural interruption to her normal fate, which required simply firmness, a good deal of will-power and energy and the proper aims to re-establish finally once more."

Miss Porter's grandmother would not face the fact that her family, in its later years, was really land-poor "in the most typical way. . . . We had been a good old family of solid wealth and property in Kentucky, Louisiana and Virginia, and we remained that in Texas, even though due to a temporary decline for the most honorable reasons, appearances were entirely to the contrary." The grandmother's "youthful confidence became matriarchal authority, a little way of knowing best about most everything, of relying upon her own experience for sole guide, and I think now she had earned her power fairly. . . . She believed it was her duty to be a stern methodical disciplinarian, and made a point of training us as she had been trained even to forbidding us to cross our knees, or to touch the back of our chair when we sat, or to speak until we were spoken to: love's labors lost utterly, for she had brought up a houseful of the worst spoiled children in seven counties, and started in again hopefully with a long series of motherless grandchildren. . . . who were to be the worst spoiled of any." She also believed that "inappropriate conduct was bad manners, bad manners were bad morals, and bad morals led to bad manners, and there you were, ringed with fire, and no way out."

Miss Porter concludes, "She was an individual being if ever I knew one, and yet she never did or said anything to make herself conspicuous; there are no strange stories to tell, no fantastic gestures," even though "she rode horseback at a gallop until the year of her death," and "her sons had to restrain her from an engineering project" when she "wished to deflect the course of a small river which was encroaching on her land in Louisiana. . . . In a family full of willful eccentrics and head-strong characters and unpredictable histories, her presence was singularly free from peaks and edges and the kind of color that leaves a trail of family anecdotes. She left the lingering perfume and the airy shimmer of grace about her memory."

And there are many other superficial connections between Miranda and Miss Porter. Miranda's age is mentioned three times, in *The Grave, Old Mortality,* and *Pale Horse, Pale Rider,* and in each instance we can make out that she must have been born in 1894, the year of Miss Porter's own birth. Again like her creator, Miranda was born in Texas. And Miss Porter herself suffered from the flu in 1918, and attempted to translate the experience of meeting death, as she has testified in the interview I have mentioned, into words.

But connections of this kind are likely to take us away from the real point, rather than bring us closer to it. The point lies, I believe, in the fact that the Miranda stories, taken together, represent Miss Porter's finest achievement. When Miranda's story is pieced together from the fragments in which it has been told, as I have tried to do, we come close, perhaps, to the novel which Miss Porter has not written. The story is composed, largely, of two contrapuntal themes: the Grand-mother, whose life begins in middle age, in tragedy and fortitude, and Miranda herself, whose life begins in early youth and culminates in the same tragedy and fortitude with which her Grandmother's had begun. The story comes full circle, in other words, and I think we may safely assume that Miranda's existence will be as joyless as her grand-mother's, but no less substantial or meaningful.

More important still, Miranda and her grandmother are individuals who have lived, like Miss Porter, amidst a world always falling to pieces. They are crushed only by the monstrous and impersonal forces of their times, and not any innate lack of character. And when we turn to Miss Porter's other stories and novelettes, we will see still another signifi-cance in the Miranda chronicles: they have a pastoral, nearly idyllic quality when we set them against the horror and violence of modern life which we encounter in some of Miss Porter's other work. Both Miranda and her Grandmother have firm moral values and instinctive feelings of right which have come to them from the stability of the past, however much Miranda may reject it.

Then, too, as will be plain in some others of Miss Porter's stories, the individual and the soul are often not spared in modern life, whereas Miranda and her Grandmother, however tragic their destiny, remained alive themselves and became better women for it. They represent en-durance in the face of the "majestic and terrible failure of the life of man in the Western world." They are, after all, among those whom the pale horse and the pale rider of the song Miranda sang with Adam, "spared to mourn."

THE NOVELETTES

Edmund Wilson, in his estimate of Katherine Anne Porter, speaks of "her conception of a natural human spirit," and he continues:

If the meaning of these stories is elusive, it is because this essential spirit is so hard to isolate or pin down. It is peculiar to Louisianians in Texas, yet one misses it in a boarding house in Berlin. It is the special personality of a woman, yet it is involved with international issues. It evades all the most admirable moralities, it escapes through the social net, and it resists the tremendous oppressions of national bankruptcies and national wars. It is outlawed, driven underground, exiled; it becomes rather unsure of itself and may be able, as in *Pale Horse, Pale Rider*, to assert itself only in the delirium that lights up at the edge of death to save Miranda from extinction by war flu. It suffers often from a guilty conscience, knowing too well its moral weakness; but it can also rally bravely if vaguely in vindication of some instinct of its being which seems to point towards justice and truth.[52]

We have seen how Miranda received this "natural human spirit" from her grandmother, and how it eventually brought her to the kind of tragedy with which her grandmother had begun. In Miss Porter's four other longer narratives, this same spirit appears in a different light; in three of them it is being done to death by hostile forces the meaning of which it cannot comprehend, and in the fourth it is preserved only after its value has been appreciated. Of these four, *The Cracked Looking-Glass* seems to stand apart, for *Noon Wine, Hacienda* and *The Leaning Tower* bear marked resemblances to one another and to *Pale Horse, Pale Rider*.

We can see clearly, in these novelettes, what Miss Porter means when she writes, in her foreword to *Flowering Judas*, that "most of the energies of my mind and spirit have been spent in the effort to grasp the meaning of those threats (of world catastrophe), to trace them to their sources and to understand the logic of this majestic and terrible failure of the life of man in the Western world." For in *Noon Wine, The Leaning Tower,* and *Hacienda,* the private world of the individual is ruthlessly and senselessly invaded from without, much as Miranda's and Adam's world, in *Pale Horse, Pale Rider,* was destroyed by the harsh impersonality of war and disease.

Both *The Leaning Tower* and *Hacienda* deal with political concepts, not as they are mirrored in the headlines or in the movements of troops, but only as their mysterious, destructive force is felt by the individual. Close readings of both stories will reveal how deliberately Miss Porter has kept these political and historical threats vague and ambiguous. In each story they are felt but never formulated by the individual center of consciousness. In *The Leaning Tower,* this particular method appears at its best. A young American artist, Charles Upton, is residing in Berlin at the end of 1931, and everything is presented to us in the light in which it appears to him; we share his experience, in all its complexity and mystery, and, at its end, we have all the horror and corruption of the rising tide of Nazism. This reveals itself, however, only in details and attitudes, and always in relation to the human personality at its center. Not once in the whole story is there an overt reference to the course of German political history.

In evoking the atmosphere of Berlin, Miss Porter relies upon certain kinds of details which have a cumulative effect upon Charles Upton. Two days after Christmas, he sets out to look for new living quarters:

> The streets were full of young people, lean and tough, boys and girls dressed alike in leather jackets or a kind of uniform blue ski suit, who whizzed about the streets on bicycles without a glance at the windows. Charles saw them carrying skis on their shoulders, shouting and laughing in groups, getting away to the mountains over the weekend. He watched them enviously; maybe if he stayed on long enough he would know some of them, he would be riding a bicycle and going away for the skiing, too. It seemed unlikely, though.[53]

He notices a group of people standing in front of an overdressed window full of hams and pigs, variously and luxuriously displayed:

> They resembled the most unkind caricatures of themselves, but they were the kind of people that Holbein and Durer and Urs Graf had drawn, too: not vaguely, but positively like, their late-medieval faces full of hallucinated malice and a kind of sluggish but intense cruelty that worked its way up from their depths slowly through the layers of helpless gluttonous fat.[54]

Even the prostitutes had their peculiar difference:

> These reserved-looking professional women, almost as regimented as soldiers in uniform, roused in him uneasy curiosity and distrust.[55]

And, in his search for new rooms, Charles learns

> A wholesome terror of landladies in that city. They were smiling faces, famished wolves, slovenly housecats, mere tigers, hyenas, furies, harpies: and sometimes worst of all they were sodden melancholy human beings who carried the history of their disasters in their faces, who all but wept when they saw him escape, as if he carried their last hopes with him.[56]

Meanwhile, the people with whom he comes into contact begin to oppress and frighten Charles quite as much as the atmosphere of the city itself, so that the details of *The Leaning Tower* form a kind of counterpoint, in which the dreary climate of Berlin is related to the sickness of some of its inhabitants. We are told, for example, that Charles leaves his first *pension* to save money, but also to escape from

> A yellow-faced woman and an ill-tempered looking fat man (who) were the proprietors, and (who) seemed to be in perpetual conspiracy of some sort before the open linen closets, in a corner of the dining-room, along the halls, or over the account books behind a varnished desk in the lobby.[57]

Signing a three month lease on new quarters, Charles begins to feel the effect of his observations at the same time that he cannot mark the real source of his unease:

> He could not see the end of those three months. He felt a blind resentment all the more deep because it could have no particular object, and helpless as if he had let himself be misled by bad advice. Vaguely but in the most ghastly sort of way, he felt that someone he trusted had left him in the lurch, and of course, that was nonsense...[58]

The doom which Charles feels all around him in Berlin is of a far more tenuous kind than that represented by the flu which nearly brought death to Miranda. The evil in *The Leaning Tower* is insidious, pervasive, and indefinite, and, if it is more abstract than the evil of *Pale Horse, Pale Rider* or *Noon Wine*, it is no less destructive. It is, however, a social and political, rather than individual, evil, capable of destroying a whole society. This, of course, is why Charles Upton is unable to put his finger on just *what* disturbs him in Berlin.

The ambiguity of this evil is embodied in the symbol from which the story derives its title: a little plaster cast of the Leaning Tower of Pisa, which, upon arriving at his new lodgings, Charles carelessly takes in his hand and breaks. Fumbling in embarrassment and anger, he apologizes and asks his landlady, Rosa Reichl, if he may replace it, but she immediately assures him that he cannot, since " 'it was a souvenir of the Italian journey,' " referring to her once prosperous and splendid past.

But it is a dueling scar which suddenly illuminates for Charles the moral desolation of the Berliners whom he meets. The scar is borne by one of his fellow-lodgers, Hans, a young student at the University, who has incurred it deliberately as a proof of valor. When another lodger, looking at the slowly healing wound, says, " 'It's doing very well,' "

> "It will last," said Hans. Over his face spread an expression very puzzling to Charles. It was there like a change of light, slow and deep, with no perceptible movement of eyelids or face muscles. It rose from within in the mysterious place where Hans really lived, and it was amazing arrogance, pleasure, inexpressible vanity and self-satisfaction.[59]

Because this expression "rose from within," and because it occurs with "no perceptible movement," it is like the whole atmosphere of Berlin, something felt but not understood, something forceful but without definite traces. Charles, thinking about the wound and the man who bears it, finds himself groping towards the real significance of this scar:

> But what *kind* of man would stand up in cold blood and let another man split his face to the teeth just for the hell of it? And then ever after to wear the wound with a look of self-satisfaction, with everybody knowing how he had got it? And you were supposed to admire him for that. Charles had liked Hans on sight, but there was something he wouldn't know about him if they both lived for a thousand years; it was something you were, or were not, and Charles rejected that wound, the reason why it existed, and everything that made it possible, then and there, simply because there were no conditions for acceptance in his mind.[60]

What the details and symbols of *The Leaning Tower* really illustrate, however, is the intense and meaningful selectivity of Miss Porter's art. No one personality dominates the story, just as no one object overshadows the scene, but, at the conclusion of the story, both the people and the dismal city merge, and the vague threat which Charles has felt all along suddenly translates itself into the plaster cast of the Leaning Tower. Here we see Miss Porter's own sense of disaster functioning in the consciousness of her protagonist. Charles, attending with the three other young men from his *pension* a New Year's Eve celebration at a small cabaret, grows angry and fearful listening to their truculent discussions of race and war. He waves to a beautiful German model,

And even at the moment, like the first symptoms of some fatal sickness, there stirred in him a most awful premonition of disaster, and his thoughts, blurred with drink and strangeness and the sound of half-understood tongues and the climate of remembered wrongs and hatreds, revolved dimly around vague remembered tales of Napoleon and Genghis Khan and Attila the Hun and all the Caesars and Alexander the Great and the dim Pharoahs and lost Babylon. He felt helpless, undefended, looked at the three strange faces near him and decided not to drink any more, for he must not be drunker than they; he trusted none of them.[61]

This might be called the first climax of *The Leaning Tower*, the horrid moment of recognition when Charles sees himself "undefended," for this is the moment towards which all his vague impressions have been heading. And it is significant that, in his isolation, Charles evokes the names of all the great conquerors of the past, thus summoning up a new one in the near future, one whose name he has not yet heard, but whose coming he senses in the awful sickness of the German people. Here Miss Porter's awareness of history complements her sense of disaster; both elements, however, register themselves only in the consciousness of the individual round whom her story centers, and never in any direct author's comment. Charles Upton has been missing the spirit of humanity all through his stay in Berlin, and suddenly he realizes what a dire threat its absence constitutes to him: it presages an actual and imminent disaster. His private world has been invaded as swiftly and surely as Miranda's, but less dramatically and more vaguely, since malice and vulgar nationalism, frustration and race hatred, are often less concrete than war flu and a dead lover. But both Miranda's tragedy and Charles Upton's horror spring from contemporary history; they are the result of those hostile elements, only dimly perceived in the order of the world, which spell death for the individual plan for happiness.

In the second climax in *The Leaning Tower*, all Charles' diverse impressions merge in the leading symbol of the story—the plaster cast of the Leaning Tower which Charles has accidentally broken. When Charles returns to his room in the early hours of the New Year, he is feeling quite drunk as he begins to prepare for bed:

As he fumbled with his pajamas, his eyes swam about in his head, seeing first one thing and then another, but none of it familiar, nothing that was his. He did notice at last that the Leaning Tower seemed to be back, sitting now safely behind the glass of the corner cabinet. By a roundabout way he brought himself across the room to the Tower. It was there, all right, and it was mended pretty obviously, it would never be the same. But for Rosa, poor old woman, he supposed it was better than nothing. . . . Leaning, suspended, perpetually ready to fall but never falling quite, the venturesome little object—a mistake in the first place, a whimsical pain in the neck, really, towers shouldn't lean in the first place; a curiosity, like those cupids falling off the roof—yet had some kind of meaning in Charles' mind. Well, what? He tousled his hair and rubbed his eyes and then his whole head and yawned himself almost inside out. What had the silly little thing reminded him of before? There was an answer if he could think what it was, but this was not the time. But just the same, there was something terribly urgent at work, in him or around him, he could not tell which. There was something perishable but threatening, uneasy, hanging over his head or stirring angrily, dangerously at his back. If he couldn't find out now what it was that troubled him so in this place, maybe he would never know. He stood there feeling his drunkenness as a pain and a weight on him, unable to think clearly but feeling what he had never known before, an infernal desolation of the spirit, the chill and the knowledge of death in him.62

Like *The Leaning Tower*, the whole rotten structure of German society is hanging over Charles, ready to fall; and we now know how fully his premonition of disaster was justified. What Miss Porter has succeeded in capturing here is nothing less than the huge and public disasters of her time, their mysterious and terrible nature rendered clear and meaningful by the poetry of her prose and through the medium of Charles Upton's consciousness. Miss Porter's characters, like those of Henry James, are armed with the imagination of horror, an apprehensive sense of the hidden meaning lurking within or without the surfaces of life.

Hacienda, like *The Leaning Tower*, deals with political issues, and only by implication. But its method is much less concrete than that of *The Leaning Tower*, and its meaning is at once more general and less clear. *Hacienda* presents roughly the same pattern as *The Leaning Tower* and *Noon Wine*: the private world of the individual is again invaded and destroyed from without. But unlike *Noon Wine* or *The Leaning Tower*, which are observed and dramatized from within the characters themselves, *Hacienda* is narrated in the first person, and its narrator makes no effort to go beyond the surface of any given situation; instead of getting the actual *effect* on the person involved, we are given only the narrator's *impression* of it. Furthermore, the narrator has no integral function in the story itself, makes no comment on it, and seems to serve mainly as reporter. *Hacienda*, in fact, has no real plot in comparison to any of Miss Porter's other longer fictions. Its central issue revolves round a Mexican peon who kills his sister in a fit of jealous rage and is taken to jail, and the responsibility for his action is connected with the currents of history which, totally uncomprehended by the peon himself, are merging around him. These currents are represented by a group of Russian communists attempting to make a propaganda movie on the grounds of the vast feudal hacienda, the American business manager of the enterprise, and the wealthy and anachronistic owners of the hacienda itself. We are not present when the murder takes place and are only told that it has happened. Much of the latter part of *Hacienda* is taken up with the owner's efforts to secure his peon's freedom from prison. These efforts are largely unsuccessful, since they depend on a bribe that Don Genaro, the owner, does not want to pay, and, at the end of the story, Dona Julia, his wife, says of the peon, " 'It is quite possible he may not come back.' "

It should be seen from this that any interest we might have in the peon himself is likely to be of a secondary order, and I suspect that this has been Miss Porter's purpose. The narrator, an American woman and a writer, seems most interested in the quality and the kinds of the people involved, in one fashion or another, with the movie: the anxious, unstable Kennerly, who represents a group of individuals financing the Russians; the Communists themselves, Andreyev, Stepanov, and Uspensky; Don Genaro and Dona Julia, whose marriage itself· exists as precariously as the superannuated hacienda on which the manufacture of pulque provides them with their wealth; Betancourt, the Mexican government's advisor to the Russians; Don Carlos, a once popular songwriter, now a failure, whom Betancourt upbraids unmercifully for his failure to become a follower of Universal Harmony. Miss Porter's, or, more accurately, her narrator's purpose in dealing with these people seems to be largely satirical; but it is satire with a tragic edge since, among themselves, these people are responsible for the peon's destruction. They represent the corruption on the one hand, and the confusion on the other, of modern social and political history; and it is in this sense that they are directly connected with the peon, who, we are led to believe, would never have murdered his sister had he not been caught in their midst.

Nowhere else is Miss Porter's analysis of the destructive force in modern life quite so tenuous; and, while I have said that I believe this is a part of her purpose, *Hacienda* does seem to lack the dramatic relevance of her very best work. Edmund Wilson has suggested that the actual meaning of the story lies in our being unable to say just *how* the peon comes to be victimized. We never meet him, however, and consequently we cannot have the interest in him that we have in Miranda or in Charles Upton. And the emptiness revealed in all the people in *Hacienda*, though pointed and sad in its implications, is not likely to disturb us as powerfully as the atmosphere of Berlin.

If *Hacienda* falls slightly below the high level of Miss Porter's usual performance, however, *Noon Wine* ranks with the best of her fiction. It is the most dramatic of all her novelettes, and for its sustained emotional intensity, it equals *Pale Horse, Pale Rider*. And, again like *Pale Horse, Pale Rider*, it is a tragedy. *Noon Wine* is another variation on the now familiar theme of the invasion of the private world by the reasonless forces of society at large; and just as *Hacienda* is Miss Porter's most nebulous statement of her theme, *Noon Wine* is her most concrete. Nowhere else in her fiction are the mysterious forces so hostile to the individual quite so succinctly dramatized as they are in the character of Mr. Hatch; and nowhere else is the individual's resistance in the face of the unknown quite so heroic as Mr. Thompson's. Much of the drama in *Noon Wine* derives from the taut confrontation of dissimilar types which we have in the long, carefully understated scene between Mr. Hatch and Mr. Thompson, and from the fact that the pawn at stake between them is another human being—Mr. Helton. One possible view of the story would be that of a moral triangle of which each of the three men forms a corner. The triangle, of course, is completely destroyed, but, significantly enough, each man dies in his own way: Mr. Helton from shock and fright and desolation, Mr. Hatch the victim of a most accidental kind of murder, and Mr. Thompson, the hero of the story, a suicide.

The questions which *Noon Wine* raises in our minds are primarily two: we must understand just what *kind* of hero Mr. Thompson is, and we must search for the real nature of his tragedy. Miss Porter points the way to the answers to both of these questions. When Mr. Helton first comes to the Thompson's farm, he meets in the owner "a noisy proud man who held his neck so straight his whole face stood level with his Adam's apple, and the whiskers continued down his neck and disappeared into a black thatch under his open collar. . . . He was just fetching a mouthful of juice to squirt again when the stranger came around the corner and stopped." In arranging to employ Mr. Helton on the farm, Mr. Thompson maintains a false bravado which he raises to cover his own sense of inadequacy, and begins "to laugh and shout his way through the deal."

If Mr. Thompson is not quite a whole man within himself, it soon develops that in Mr. Helton he has found his proper complement, for the farm begins to be a small success as Mr. Helton takes over its management:

The Thompsons did not grow rich, but they kept out of the poor house, as Mr. Thompson was fond of saying, meaning he had got a little foothold in spite of Ellie's poor health, and unexpected weather, and strange declines in market prices, and his own mysterious handicaps which weighed him down. Mr. Helton was the hope and the prop of the family . . . .[63]

Mr. Thompson thinks of himself, and not of Mr. Helton, as having got "a little foothold," but he is able, nevertheless, to recognize "his own mysterious handicaps which weighed him down." These handicaps are as vague to us as they are to him, but we realize that they are a part of his general sense of not being able to achieve his potential, whatever that might be. These same handicaps, however, operate to keep us from thinking of Mr. Thompson as a hero, and we do not begin to see him in that role until, after nine years have passed, he confronts an ambiguous but very real horror in the person of Mr. Homer T. Hatch:

He wasn't exactly a fat man. He was more like a man who had been fat recently.

His skin was baggy and his clothes were too big for him, and he somehow looked like a man who should be fat, ordinarily, but who might have just got over a spell of sickness. Mr. Thompson didn't take to his looks at all, he couldn't say why.[64]

The long scene which follows between Mr. Thompson and Mr. Hatch is one of Miss Porter's most brilliant. Mr. Hatch, in revealing why he has come after Mr. Helton, also reveals his own manner of preying on unfortunate human beings:

"Fact is, I might need your help in the little matter I've got on hand, but it won't cost you any trouble. Now, this Mr. Helton here, like I tell you, he's a dangerous escaped loonatic, you might say. Now fact is, in the last twelve years or so I musta rounded up twenty-odd escaped loonatics, besides a couple of escaped convicts that I just run into by accident, like. I don't make a business of it, but if there's a reward, and there usually is a reward of course, I get it. It amounts to a tidy little sum in the long run, but that ain't the main question. Fact is, I'm for law and order, I don't like to see lawbreakers and loonatics at large. It ain't the place for them."[65]

Mr. Thompson can hardly accept Mr. Hatch's story; he begins to defend Mr. Helton; but Mr. Hatch seems, in his maddening manner, to turn everything Mr. Thompson says inside out. Mr. Thompson decides he had better get rid of Mr. Hatch as quickly as possible, but he wonders how.

And suddenly we come to the crux of Mr. Thompson's tragedy. When Mr. Hatch brings out a pair of handcuffs, Mr. Thompson becomes all the more frightened, but he has an obscure, nibbling feeling that he does not really grasp what is happening. He raises his voice and orders Mr. Hatch off his property, and then something happens that Mr. Thompson will never understand the rest of his life:

He took a step towards the fat man, who backed off, shrinking, "Try it, try it, go ahead!" and then something happened that Mr. Thompson tried hard afterwards to piece together in his mind, and in fact it never did come straight. He saw the fat man with his long bowie knife in his hand, he saw Mr. Helton come round the corner on the run, his long jaw dropped, his arms swinging, his eyes wild. Mr. Helton came in between them, fists doubled up, then stopped short, glaring at the fat man, his big frame seemed to collapse, he trembled like a shied horse; and then the fat man drove at him, knife in one hand, handcuffs in the other. Mr. Thompson saw it coming, he saw the blade going into Mr. Helton's stomach, he knew he had the ax out of the log in his own hands, felt his arms go up over his head and bring the ax down on Mr. Hatch's head as if he were stunning a beef.[66]

It is at just this moment, when he is caught up in a fate that he does not and never will understand, but which he nevertheless blindly contests, that Mr. Thompson becomes tragic. All the rest of his life is to be spent in an effort to vindicate himself for having contested this fate. Though he is easily acquitted in court, he becomes all the more uneasy when he learns that Mr. Helton had been captured uninjured. Mr. Thompson had been certain he saw Mr. Hatch's knife entering Mr. Helton, and now he wonders constantly about the nature of what really happened:

He had killed Mr. Hatch and he was a murderer. That was the truth about himself that Mr. Thompson couldn't grasp, even when he said the word to himself. Why, he had not even once *thought* of killing anybody, much less Mr. Hatch, and if Mr. Helton hadn't come out so unexpectedly, hearing the row, why, then—but then, Mr. Helton had come on the run that way to help him. What he couldn't understand was what happened next. He had seen Mr. Hatch go after Mr. Helton with the knife, he had seen the point, blade up, go into Mr. Helton's stomach and slice up like you slice a hog, but when they finally caught Mr. Helton there wasn't a knife scratch on him. Mr. Thompson knew he had the ax in his own hands and felt himself lifting it, but he couldn't remember hitting Mr. Hatch. He couldn't remember it. He couldn't. He remembered only that he had been determined to stop Mr. Hatch from cutting Mr. Helton.[67]

The meaning of the knife is the clue to the nature of Mr. Thompson's tragedy. Why does Mr. Thompson believe he has seen something which he could not have seen? The knife is not an alibi, of course; it is the symbol by which Miss Porter dramatizes the confusion and unreality of the evil which suddenly overtakes Mr. Thompson, just as she dramatizes the evil itself in the strange face and manner of Mr. Hatch. And Mr. Thompson's heroism rises largely from his lack of preparation for his role, and from his spontaneous willingness to defend the light, which he equates with Mr. Helton, against the dark and Mr. Hatch. And there is a harsh and rampant impersonality in the destruction of Mr. Thompson's world which reminds us of the sickness which overtook Miranda and of the queer combination of hostile forces which Charles Upton encountered in Berlin. After all, Mr. Thompson himself is in no way responsible for either Mr. Hatch or Mr. Helton, and yet he becomes the victim of the issue between them. And Mr. Thompson becomes all the more tragic as he continues to puzzle out his lonely fate, making the rounds of his neighbors in an effort to vindicate himself even after he had been acquitted in court. Then there comes the dreadful moment when he recognizes that "the end had come":

Now, this minute, lying in the bed where he had slept with Ellie for eighteen years; under this roof where he had laid the shingles when he was waiting to get married; there as he was with his whiskers already sprouting since his shave that morning; with his fingers feeling his bony chin, Mr. Thompson felt he was a dead man. He was dead to his other life, he had got to the end of something without knowing why, and he had to make a fresh start, he did not know how. Something different was going to begin, he did not know what. It was in some way not his business. He didn't feel he was going to have much to do with it.[68]

That same night, Mr. Thompson starts out of his sleep and frightens his wife into a faint, and the last strokes of his swift, sure doom seem to be fulfilled when his sons enter their parents' room, and Mr. Thompson sees the distrust in their eyes. Not only has his mysterious fate overborne him but he now knows irrevocably that he has lost the trust of his family; he is utterly alone with the strange and incomprehensible destiny which has overtaken him. He goes to the kitchen, takes down his rifle, and walks out to the extreme limit of his property. Here he sits down against a fence and writes the note in which he tries to explain, to himself and everyone else, just what had really happened to him:

"Before Almighty God, the great judge of all before who I am about to die, I do solemnly swear that I did not take the life of Homer T. Hatch on purpose. It was done in defense of Mr. Helton. I did not aim to hit him with the ax but only to keep him off Mr. Helton. He aimed a blow at Mr. Helton who was not looking for it. It was my belief at the time that Mr. Hatch would of taken the life of Mr. Helton if I did not interfere. I have told all this to the judge and the jury and they let me off but nobody believes it. This is the only way I can prove I am not a cold blooded murderer like everybody seems to think. If I had been in Mr. Helton's place he would of done the same for me. I still think I done the only thing there was to do. My wife—"

Here Mr. Thompson breaks off, and then resumes:

"It was Homer T. Hatch who came to do wrong to a harmless man. He caused all this trouble and he deserved to die but I am sorry it was me who had to kill him."[69]

Though the source of destruction is plainly Mr. Hatch, Mr. Thompson is still fumbling for the meaning of the murder he has committed; in this final testament, is certainty that a knife had entered Mr. Helton has changed to the fact that Mr. Hatch "aimed a blow," and he can only state his belief "that Mr. Hatch would of taken the life of Mr. Helton if I did not interfere." It is precisely the ambiguity of Mr. Thompson's experience which makes it seem so universal; we can conceive of its befalling anyone. And though the evil in *Noon Wine* is so concretely embodied in Mr. Hatch, it is nonetheless a subtle and diffuse force the meaning of which man cannot completely grasp. Because Mr. Thompson follows what seems to him to be the course of right, and because he struggles so valiantly to understand and to justify his course against insurmountable odds, Mr. Thompson is heroic. But he is isolated in his heroism, and, after he has written his note, he must submit to the fate which, even now, he does not understand:

He licked the point of his pencil again, and signed his full name carefully, folded the paper and put it in his inside pocket. Taking off his right shoe and sock, he set the butt of the shotgun along the ground with the twin barrels pointed towards his head. It was very awkward. He thought about this a little, leaning his head against the gun mouth. He was trembling and his head was drumming until he was deaf and blind, but he lay down flat on the earth on his side, drew the barrel under his chin and fumbled for the trigger with his great toe. That way he could work it.[70]

In the last of Miss Porter's novelettes, *The Cracked Looking-Glass*, we are a long way from tragedy, and in a world far more subdued than Miranda's, Mr. Thompson's, or Charles Upton's. Dennis and Rosaleen are an Irish couple living in Connecticut, and their story deserts the domestic scene only long enough to return to it with a renewed appreciation. By clinging tightly to her little area of security, Rosaleen escapes whatever fate the outer world might hold for her. Married to a man much older than herself, Rosaleen is driven, by the thought of his encroaching age and her knowledge that all his splendor lies in the past, when he had been a headwaiter in New York, into queer, talkative friendships with salesmen who travel the country roads. And she is obsessed by her dreams, both the superstitious, premonitory dreams she has in sleep and her particular private dream of a better life for herself. What *The Cracked Looking-Glass* really illustrates is the failure of this latter dream to sustain itself in terms of reality. Rosaleen, answering what she believes to be a summons in her dreams to a sister in Boston, sets out for that city; but she fails to find her sister and only meets instead "a scrap of a lad with freckles, his collar turned up about his ears, his red hair wilted on his forehead under his bulging cap," a destitute Irish immigrant who mistakes her impulsive sympathy for a proposition.

What Rosaleen has really learned on her trip to Boston is that the only life available to her is the one with Dennis. All her thoughts of her past, when she had been popular, capricious and good-looking, all her reminiscences of her brother, Kevin, gay and charming, who had lived with her and Dennis until she had come out against his girl friend, when he had gone off to New York, suddenly seem to drop from her, to presage no more splendid future. This meaning is reinforced by the symbol of the cracked looking-glass itself, a mirror that had hung in the house for years, cracked across its breadth and distorting the countenance of whoever looks into it, so that when Rosaleen sees herself in it, "the wavy place made her eyes broad and blurred as the palm of her hands, and she couldn't tell her nose from her mouth in the cracked seam." Significantly enough, this mirror had never bothered Dennis, but Rosaleen had decided to replace it on her trip to Boston; returning home, however, she discovers that she has forgotten all about it. Walking along a country road near her home, Rosaleen dawdles:

"Life is a dream," she said aloud, in a soft easy melancholy. "It's a mere dream." The thought and the words pleased her, and she gazed with pleasure at the loosened stones of the wall across the road, dark brown, with the thin shining coat of ice on them, in a comfortable daze until her feet began to feel chilled.

"Let me not sit here and take my death at my early time of life," she cautioned herself, getting up and wrapping her shawl carefully around her. She was thinking how this sad countryside needed some young hearts in it, and how she wished Kevin would come back. . . . That dream about her sister now, it hadn't come true at all. Maybe the dream about Kevin wasn't true either. If one dream failed on you, it would be foolish to think another mightn't fail you too; wouldn't it, wouldn't it? She smiled at Dennis sitting by the stove.[71]

Abandoning her gay and happy past, her hopeful dreams, she tells Dennis, " 'I don't put the respect on dreams that I once did,' " and he replies, " 'Maybe that's a good thing.' " Then Rosaleen notices the looking-glass, and cries out, " 'Oh, Dennis, I forgot to buy a looking-glass, I forgot it altogether.' " " 'It's a good enough glass,' " says Dennis. And Rosaleen, in accepting the crack in the looking-glass, accepts also her imperfect marriage, and returns to her life with Dennis, aged and inadequate though he might be:

"I want you to wrap up warm this bitter weather, Dennis," she told him. "With two pairs of sox and the chest protector, for if anything happened to you, whatever would become of me in this world?"

"Let's not think of it," said Dennis, shuffling his feet.

"Let's not, then," said Rosaleen. "For I could cry if you crooked a finger at me."[72]

The Cracked Looking-Glass is one of the most perfect in form and tone of Miss Porter's stories. But it focuses so completely on its narrow domestic scene that it seems, in the end, less rich in implication than Miss Porter's other long stories. Dennis and Rosaleen have none of the universal application of Miranda, Charles Upton, Mr. Thompson, or even of the Mexican peon of *Hacienda*. But *The Cracked Looking-Glass* provides an interesting variation on the familiar theme of the invasion of the individual world; the invasion here is very slight, and Rosaleen escapes from it by abandoning the dream and accepting the reality. The fundamental difference between Dennis and Rosaleen in this story and Miranda, Charles Upton, and Mr. Thompson in the others, however, is one of perception: for the Irish couple do not really question their destiny, whereas the others are constantly trying to grasp the meaning of the situations in which they find themselves. Their vision is, in the phrase of Henry James, "the religion of consciousness." Miranda, Mr. Thompson, and Charles Upton offer evidence of a kind altogether different from that of *The Cracked Looking-Glass*. The great reality for them is the all-important little human world senselessly sundered from without, its private harmony destroyed by the hostility of blind, incomprehensible forces. And in two of the stories, *Pale Horse, Pale Rider* and *Noon Wine*, that destruction is of the nature of tragedy.

THE SHORT STORIES

Besides the six novelettes and the six Miranda sketches, Katherine Anne Porter has published ten other shorter pieces of fiction. Two of these, *The Downward Path to Wisdom* and *A Day's Work*, appear in the volume, *The Leaning Tower;* the other eight are from *Flowering Judas*. These short stories show a much greater range of attitude, tone and substance than the novelettes and the Miranda pieces, and this is possibly why, taken all together, they are less consistent in their levels of achievement. In some of them, Miss Porter's pervasive theme of the senseless destruction of the individual is rendered in a new and moving form: in *The Downward Path to Wisdom*, for instance, the private world is that of a four-year-old boy and the destructive elements it encounters are represented by the incomprehensible behavior of adults: in another, *Flowering Judas*, a young girl who has devoted herself wholeheartedly to the revolutionary movement in Mexico suddenly discovers that she is a traitor to herself as well as to the ranks of the oppressed, and that she must identify herself with Judas rather than with any liberator of mankind.

Flowering Judas is certainly one of Miss Porter's most beautifully written stories, and, in its subject matter at least, it invites comparison with *Hacienda*. Like the latter story, *Flowering Judas* is very tenuously assembled; it conveys a mood rather than tells a story, but the mood itself leads to a climax of self-revelation when the girl, Laura, suddenly sees through the maze of intrigue in which she has been caught. Like the heroes and heroines of the novelettes, Laura sees her world fall to pieces through no essential fault of her own, but because of the corruption and dissimulation on which it rests. And Braggioni is as concrete, though perhaps not as human, a symbol of that corruption as is Mr. Hatch in *Noon Wine*. What *Flowering Judas* suggests so powerfully is the treacherous capacity of the individual to do wrong even when armed with the firmest intentions of doing right; and the story itself, like the modern history of which it is an instance, indicates this in the light of the tragic course of contemporary political events, in which so many noble concepts have led to so much horror and oppression. *Flowering Judas*, like *Hacienda* and *The Leaning Tower*, shows us how little Miss Porter's political sense can be separated from her acute perception of individual tragedy; in all three of these stories, in fact, the particular social and historical disaster is recorded only through its effect on an individual caught in its center. Miss Porter's political sense is strong precisely because she sees the important connection between the hope of the individual and the course of the mass. And Laura, in *Flowering Judas,* illustrates this connection much more powerfully than does the poor peon of *Hacienda.* If Laura is finally forced to brand herself a traitor, it is not through a series of steps or events which she can comprehend, but only because of the blind upheaval of the social order in which she is inextricably involved; and, just as Laura finds herself so abruptly in the wrong, so do revolutions.

Another story, *Rope,* which verges on the *tour de force* because of its mastery of the adroit, insinuating tone, is an astonishing illustration of how a minor difference of opinion can develop into a quarrel which reveals all the cracks in a marriage. The young couple in *Rope* hardly realize the meaning of their charges and counter-charges, for they are completely caught up in the mechanism of their quarrel, but, all the while, the sickness of their marriage magnifies itself in their inadvertent accusations. *Rope* is primarily notable for the control of its tone; read in one way, it is a diverting social comedy with a happy end, and, read in another, it is a disturbing revelation of the malice stored beneath the blandest surfaces of life.

In *He,* we have the story of a mother whose whole life lies in her feeble-minded son, and whose final tragedy comes to her when she is forced to put him in the county home. Mrs. Whipple is not to be blamed for the fact that her son is a mental defective, but she is altogether committed to Him (throughout the story, the son is referred to only by capitalized personal pronouns) both because she loves him and because he is absolutely dependent upon her. The pathetic ending of the story is implicit in its beginning, since life for Him, and for his mother, cannot have a happy outcome, especially given the added stress of the Whipple's desperate poverty. But the real significance of Mrs. Whipple's life lies in her effort to make a life for her son, little though she can help; otherwise his going off to the county home would be a solution to a pressing problem rather than a grim tragedy in a mother's life.

Among Miss Porter's shorter stories, it is perhaps *Maria Concepcion* which is her most moving and eloquent variation on the destructive theme. *Maria Concepcion* is a simple, direct story (the first Miss Porter ever finished, we learn from her preface to *Flowering Judas*) of a young Mexican peasant woman who kills the girl who threatens to steal her husband from her, and thus wins back her husband and restores her universe to order. In *Maria Concepcion,* however, the destruction proceeds from the protagonist herself, and it is only after a cold act of murder that her world assumes its former balance. But this murder does not disturb the Mexican peasant girl who commits it and who regards it as merely something she has to do in order to retain her peace and happiness. The story closes on a note of peaceful domesticity, a strange contrast to the violent means by which the peace has been obtained.

Maria Concepcion could hear Juan's breathing. The sound vapored from the low doorway, calmly; the house seemed to be resting after a burdensome day. She breathed, too, very slowly and quietly, each inspiration saturating her with repose. The child's light, faint breath was a mere shadowy moth of sound in the silver air. The night, the earth around her, seemed to swell and recede together with a limitless, unhurried, benign breathing. She drooped and closed her eyes, feeling the slow rise and fall within her own body. She did not know what it was, but it eased her all through. Even as she was falling asleep, head bowed over the child, she was still aware of a strange, wakeful happiness.[73]

So Maria Concepcion returns to the elemental existence of the earth she loves and understands, and the savage primitivism of which she is herself an expression. She has done so only at the cost of another's bloodshed, however, and we are thus brought very close once again to the forces that indicate the "terrible failure of the life of man in the Western world." *Maria Concepcion* illustrates the plight of an individual driven to take the life of another, and one who can do so without raising any questions of morality, but simply as a means of gaining a desired end. It is also a profound statement of how disastrously private worlds may collide.

Another of Miss Porter's stories, *The Jilting of Granny Weatherall,* brings us very close to *Pale Horse, Pale Rider,* which it resembles in its concern with, and representation of, death. Unlike Miranda, Granny Weatherall is an old woman whose life has been lived, and who succumbs to death at her appointed time. But the same Granny Weatherall, lying on her sickbed, passes back and forth from the real world of the living to the phantoms and shadows of death much as did Miranda. Miranda's real tragedy lay ahead of her, however, and waited for her recovery to reveal itself, whereas Granny Weatherall's tragedy lay, like all of her life, in the past. She had once been jilted right at the altar, and this had been the great and unforgotten pain of her whole life. And if Granny Weatherall resembles Miranda, in other respects, at least, she resembles Miranda's grandmother still more: like the Grandmother, Granny Weatherall has long been the stabilizing force in a large family, but this position of authority has not dulled the pain of her private tragedy. If the Grandmother's heart had broken "once and for all" when her two sons stole away to eat sugar cane, so had Granny Weatherall's when her fiance failed to appear for her wedding. And now, waiting for death one moment and deluding herself into further of life the next, befuddled by the appearance of her sons and daughters and escaping into her interior visions of death, Granny Weatherall feels not the whole of her life within her, but only its greatest pain. It is her lost lover whom she sees most clearly, and the awful hurt he caused her which she now feels so deeply:

Yes, she had changed her mind after sixty years and she would like to see George. I want you to find George. Find him and be sure to tell him I forgot him. I want him to know I had a husband just the same and my children and my house like any other woman. A good house too and a good husband that I loved and fine children out of him. Tell him I was given back everything he took away and more. Oh, no, Oh, God, no, there was something else besides the house and the man and the children. Oh, surely they were not all? What was it? Something not given back.[74]

At the story's conclusion, Granny's death merges with her jilting. Granny's eyes are focused on the light from the bedside lamp which

drew into a tiny point in the center of her brain, it flickered and winked like an eye, quietly it fluttered and dwindled. Granny lay curled down within herself, amazed and watchful, staring at the point of light that was herself; her body was now only a deeper mass of shadow in an endless darkness and this darkness would curl around the light and swallow it up. God, give a sign!

For the second time there was no sign. Again no bridegroom and the priest in the house. She could not remember any other sorrow because this grief wiped them all away. Oh, no, there's nothing more cruel than this—I'll never forgive it. She stretched herself with a deep breath and blew out the light.[57]

Granny's death reveals the fortitude which has carried her through life, and her absolute refusal to capitulate to a private sorrow which has nonetheless dominated her life.

What these short stories more and more disclose, and what brings them so close to the novelettes, is the terrible predicament of the individual in the modern world. Miss Porter, in all her fiction, is concerned with the "natural human spirit" of which Edmund Wilson writes, and it is perhaps indicative of the importance of this spirit, for her particular art as well as for humanity, that the two stories which deal with its absence rather than with its life and death, seem to be the least impressive of all Miss Porter's work. *A Day's Work* and *That Tree* are carried off at their author's customary high level of technique, but they fail in their final effect, I believe, simply because we are not likely to care about the people with whom they deal in the way that we care for Miranda or Mr. Thompson, Granny Weatherall or the little boy in *The Downward Path to Wisdom*. In *A Day's* Work, we meet the Hallorans, a middle-aged Irish couple living in New York. Once, in the past, Mr. Halloran might have cut a small career for himself in the petty ward politics of the city, had not his wife objected to all the politicians he knew, and to one in particular, the boss McCorkery. In the meantime, McCorkery has risen steadily in the world while Mr. Halloran has gone continually down, to the point where he has gone on relief and his wife is taking in washing. Now, in mute despair, Halloran seems to have come under his wife's morbid, depleting power and, on the day round which the story is constructed, he makes one last attempt to break with his bad luck (which, of course, is synonymous with his vulgar and prententious wife) only to find himself rejected by his old friend, McCorkery, who makes him drunk and returns him home a fool to his wife. Miss Porter writes in a more colloquial vein than usual in *A Day's Work*, and her people are just as acutely portrayed as ever. But the dull melancholy of their lives communicates itself almost too well to the reader, so that in the end they seem persons of little consequence.

That Tree is an exception in more ways than one to the rest of Miss Porter's work. Here she is concerned with the pretentious person, a man who in his youth "had really wanted to be a cheerful bum lying under a tree in a good climate, writing poetry," and the failure of whose first marriage had changed him into "an important journalist, an authority on Latin-American revolutions and a best seller." The central character of *That Tree* is given no name; like the little boy in *He,* he is referred to only by the personal pronouns. But whereas *He* is a small tragedy, *That Tree* is an exercise in ironic comedy which reveals the void in which the commercial artist, or the artist who confuses the highest standards of his art with those of success, must operate; in this particular respect, it reminds us of some of Miss Porter's more stringent comments in *The Days Before.* The protagonist of *That Tree* is engaged, throughout the story, in a superficial conversation with a friend in a Mexican cafe, and the conversation reveals the talker. What we really learn is how his first wife, Miriam, who had been unable to accept his Bohemian standards when she came to Mexico to marry him, and who had left him after four years of marriage, has in reality succeeded in subjugating him to her by forcing him to abandon all the aspirations of his youth. Through two more marriages and several more years, her shadow has never deserted him, and now, a success and a hollow man as well, he is preparing to take her back. *That Tree* is Miss Porter's only real exercise in satire; it sustains the irony at which much of *Hacienda* hints. But, like *A Day's Work,* it provides us with no one with whom we can sympathize.

Magic and *Theft,* the last of the stories from *Flowering Judas,* also differ largely from the rest of Miss Porter's work. *Magic* is at most a sketch, but it is a nearly perfect thing of its kind: a narration by a lady's maid of a subtle and evil charm brought to work in a New Orleans' brothel. *Theft* is an adroit story of self-revelation. Once again we have a central character who is nameless, though this time she is a woman, a young writer living in the art world of New York in the late twenties or early thirties, who learns, when her janitress steals her purse, that there is a greater and more insidious kind of theft than that which the law courts acknowledge, and who concludes: "I was right not to be afraid of any thief but myself, who will end by leaving me nothing."

What Miss Porter is working towards in all these stories is the same kind of statement which she attains in the novelettes. She seems to be asking just what kinds of human situations and predicaments lead to frustration, hatred, destruction and defeat. In other words, she is projecting on the level of the individual consciousness a conflict for which the immediate history of the world is only a larger parallel; and in doing so she enlarges our sense of human resourcefulness and complexity.

Perhaps this is nowhere better illustrated than in *The Downward Path to Wisdom,* one of her finest and most moving stories. Unlike *Theft,*

Magic, That Tree, and some of the other shorter pieces, *The Downward Path to Wisdom* is a direct variation on four of the six novelettes. The major difference in this story lies in the fact that it is developed through the mind of a four-year-old boy. Just as Mr. Thompson, in *Noon Wine,* and Charles Upton, in *The Leaning Tower,* were never certain of just what kind of evil confronted them, but knew nonetheless that it was present, so the child Stephen, in *The Downward Path to Wisdom,* finds the universe of adults incomprehensible but recognizes its destructive power.

Stephen is a "victim" of his family, but he is altogether different from most children of this kind. At the beginning of the story, he is sent out from the confusion of his home, where his parents are quarreling desperately, to what seems the safe sanctuary of his grandmother's house. But he is to learn, through one of those small tragedies which are always insurmountable to a child, what faithlessness and disloyality exist in this house as well as his own. The threat to Stephen's little world is announced early in the story, during the quarrel between his mother and father:

The little boy had to pass his father on the way to the door. He shrank into himself when he saw the big hand raised above him. "Yes, get out of here and stay out," said Papa, giving him a little shove toward the door. It was not a hard shove, but it hurt the little boy."[76]

But the real betrayal in *The Downward Path to Wisdom* rests neither with the parents nor the grandmother, but with the grandmother's son, Stephen's Uncle David. It is David who introduces Stephen to the joys of balloons, who contests with him for the honor of blowing them up, and who is responsible for the pride Stephen feels in giving the balloons to a playmate. But it is also David who accuses Stephen of theft when he discovers that some of the balloons have been taken from their box, and who thus becomes the agent of separating the child from his grandmother and of having her send him back home.

The obscurity of adult conversation is impressed on Stephen all through the story. From the very beginning, his elders speak as if he were not present, or as if they took for granted that their meanings passed beyond him:

"Bright-looking specimen, isn't he?" asked Papa, stretching his long legs and reaching for his bathrobe. "I suppose you'll say it's my fault he's dumb as an ox."

"He's my little baby, my only baby," said Mama richly, hugging him, "and he's a dear lamb." His neck and shoulders were quite boneless in her firm embrace. He stopped chewing long enough to receive a kiss on his crumby chin. "He's sweet as clover," said Mama. The baby went on chewing.

"Look at him staring like an owl," said Papa.

Mama said, "He's an angel and I'll never get used to having him."

We'd be better off if we never *had* had him," said Papa.[77]

It is this kind of conversation which gives Stephen his sense of the threat to himself in adult relations. He overhears a Negro servant talking to his grandmother, saying, " 'all this upset all the time, and him such a baby.' " And Uncle David, after accusing him of stealing the balloons, turns to his mother and reports on his telephone call to his sister, Stephen's mother:

"It's simply in cold blood, I told her," said Uncle David. "I told her she would simply have to come and get him, and keep him. She asked me if I meant to call him a thief and I said if she could think of a more exact word I'd be glad to hear it."

"You shouldn't have said that," commented Grandma calmly.

"Why not? She might as well know the facts. . . . I suppose he can't help it," said Uncle David, stopping now in front of Stephen and dropping his chin into his collar, "I shouldn't expect too much of him, but you can't begin to early—"

"The trouble is," said Grandma, and while she spoke she took Stephen by the chin and held it up so that he had to meet her eye; she talked steadily in a mournful tone, but Stephen could not understand. She ended, "It's not just about the balloons, of course."

"It *is* about the balloons," said Uncle David angrily, "because balloons now mean something worse later. But what can you expect? His father—well, its in the blood. He—"

"That's your sister's husband you're talking about," said Grandma, "and there is no use making things worse. Besides, you don't really *know*."

"I *do know*," said Uncle David. And he talked again very fast, walking up and down. Stephen tried to understand, but the sounds were strange and floating just above his head. They were talking about his father, and they did not like him. Uncle David came and stood above Stephen and Grandma. He hunched over them with a frowning face, a long, crooked shadow from him falling across them to the wall. To Stephen he looked like his father, and he shrank against his grandma's skirts.[78]

In *The Downward Path to Wisdom*, the betrayal of Stephen is a betrayal of love to hatred and frustration. It is not precisely the fault of Uncle David or Grandma or Mama or Papa or any of the servants; it is more accurate to say that it represents a kind of tacit conspiracy on the part of his elders to defeat the forces of love and hope in the child, and to bring him to an unwise and precocious maturity. The maturity, when it comes, is one of cynicism and disillusionment; childhood is surrendered, but nothing is gained. Driving home with his mother,

Stephen began suddenly to sing to himself, a quiet, inside song so Mama would not hear. He sang his new secret; it was a comfortable, sleepy song: "I hate Papa, I hate Mama, I hate Grandma, I hate Uncle David, I hate Old Janet, I hate Marjory, I hate Papa, I hate Mama . . ."[79]

The path to wisdom is a downward one because it is also the path to despair. Stephen is really no different from most of Miss Porter's other heroes and heroines; he is a child and most of them are adults, but they have all retained the childishness of hope and of a belief in the essential goodness and dignity of man, whatever their ages. And this is why they matter to us, and why they have something important to say. It is also why they frequently become tragic when they contest their senseless, extravagant fates, when they apprehend the twisted and hideous evil behind the closed doors of society. And whether the society be primitive, as in *Maria Concepcion,* or nobly traditional, as in the Miranda chronicle, or rigid and utilitarian, as in *The Leaning Tower,* or poverty-stricken and narrowly domestic, as in *He,* it is never fool-proof against the dire threats of the half-grasped and unadmitted human motive.

Miss Porter is passionately concerned with the common man in a day when he has become the special property of the proletarian writers and the wielders of shibboleths. But she is neither of these, of course; she is simply a firm and delicate artist who has recognized, and drama-tized the lonely plight of the individual caught in a destiny for which nothing has prepared him. The various ways of meeting this destiny form the specific subjects of most of the stories and novelettes; it may be questioned and contested, as Mr. Thompson questions and contests it in *Noon Wine;* it may be submitted to without heroism and in tacit despair, as Mr. Halloran submits to it in *A Day's Work;* it may be beau-tifully and tragically survived, as Miranda survives it in *Pale Horse, Pale Rider,* and as her grandmother survives it in *The Old Order;* it may be fought by an act of violence, as in *Maria Concepcion;* it may result simply in a blinding flash of self-revelation, as in *Theft* or *Flowering Judas;* it may be so completely incomprehensible as to be beyond fighting, as Charles Upton finds it in *The Leaning Tower;* it may be held at bay during a lifetime and defied even in death, as in *The Jilting of Granny Weatherall;* or it may be met and surrendered to very early in life, as in *The Downward Path to Wisdom.*

When Miss Porter's stories and novelettes are read all together, as I have had occasion to read them, their meaning emerges with all the unity we expect from a novel. Her people are a small and noble com-pany for whom an abiding faith in humanity has been a religion; and their bleak fates and tragedies have resulted from the loss of illusion through the experience of reality. The "natural human spirit" which they represent is the very substance of life and endurance, hope and belief. Without it, we have a very dismal world indeed, as stories like *That Tree* and *A Day's Work* seem to indicate; and with it, we have the nobility of Miranda in *Pale Horse, Pale Rider* and of Mr. Thompson in *Noon Wine.* It is a spirit as universal as life itself, and it can be threat-ened and even killed in Berlin or Mexico or in a country house in Con-necticut or on a small south Texas farm: and it can be defended and preserved in Kentucky and Louisiana, in tiny, humble homes, and amid the antiseptic rooms of hospitals.

This same spirit is not, of course, always triumphant, but it is vigorous and splendid even in defeat. It is based on the desperate, childish, enduring hope for the best in life and in human relations. It is preserved and defended through love and loyalty and fortitude. It is a very lonely /spirit, often exposed to the onslaughts of the evil and the vulgar. But it can find lovely and durable expression in an act of faith in human solidarity.

All Miss Porter's real heroes and heroines have this spirit in common; it separates them from the Kennerlys, the Mr. Hatchs, and the Hans. It is a very real and loftly ideal of which they never lose sight and for which they expend the very substance of their lives. And yet it is an ideal which is over and over again done to death in the private and public struggles for survival. Those who possess it constantly advance the cause of humanity at the same time that they are inevitably disillusioned by the sudden knowledge of the evil in man. It is the horrible shock for which they have never been prepared, and their very high-mindedness often keeps them from understanding the nature of their destinies. That is why, for them, the path to wisdom is indeed a downward one; and it is also why they matter, and persist, and endure, and why they are important to all of us who wish to continue believing and struggling and surviving.

Footnotes to Profile of an Artist

1 Reprinted in *Classics and Commercials* by Edmund Wilson (New York, 1950), pp. 219-223.
2 Stanley Edgar Hyman, *The Armed Vision* (New York, 1948), p. 45.
3 Katherine Anne Porter, *The Days Before* (New York, 1952), "Three Statements about Writing," pp. 129-131.
4 *The New York Times Book Review*, April 14, 1940, reprinted in *Writers and Writing*, by Robert Van Gelder (New York, 1945).
5 Katherine Anne Porter, Forword to *The Days Before*, p. vii.
6 Henry James, *The Art of the Novel* (New York, 1953), p. 5.
7 Katherine Anne Porter, *The Days Before*, "Three Statements about Writing," pp. 123-124.
8 Edmund Wilson, *Classics and Commercials*, p. 219.
9 Katherine Anne Porter, *The Days Before*, "Three Statements about Writing," p. 132.
10 *Ibid.*, " 'It is Hard to Stand in the Middle,' " p. 74.
11 *Ibid.*, "Virginia Woolf," p. 113.
12 *Ibid.*, "Virginia Woolf," p. 115.
13 *Ibid.*, "On a Criticism of Thomas Hardy," p. 35.
14 *Ibid.*, "Reflections on Willa Cather," p. 71.
15 *Ibid.*, "Reflections on Willa Cather," pp. 72-73.
16 *Ibid.*, "E. M. Forster," p. 118.
17 *Ibid.*, "Orpheus in Purgatory," p. 92.
18 *Ibid.*, " 'The Laughing Heat of the Sun,' " pp. 97-98.
19 *Ibid.*, " 'It is Hard to Stand in the Middle,' " p. 78.
20 *Ibid.*, "The Art of Katherine Mansfield," p. 86.
21 *Ibid.*, "Three Statements about Writing," p. 129.
22 *Ibid.*, "Three Statements about Writing," pp. 127-128.
23 *Ibid.*, "American Statement: 4 July 1942," p. 195.
24 *Ibid.*, "The Future Is Now," p. 202.
25 *Ibid.*, "Quetzalcoatl," p. 267.

Footnotes to Miranda

26 Katherine Anne Porter, *The Leaning Tower* (New York, 1944), "The Source," pp. 3-10.
27 *Ibid.*, "The Old Order," pp. 35-56.
28 *Ibid.*, "The Grave," pp. 69-78.
29 *Ibid.*, "The Circus," pp. 21-29.
30 Katherine Anne Porter, *Pale Horse, Pale Rider* (New York, 1939), "Old Mortality," pp. 3-89.
31 *Ibid.*, pp. 87-89.
32 Katherine Anne Porter, *Pale Horse, Pale Rider*, "Pale Horse, Pale Rider," pp. 179-180.
33 *Ibid.*, p. 181.
34 *Ibid.*, p. 200.
35 *Ibid.*, p. 205.
36 *Ibid.*, pp. 218-219.
37 *Ibid.*, p. 225.
38 *Ibid.*, p. 227.
39 *Ibid.*, p. 231.
40 *Ibid.*, p. 232.
41 *Ibid.*, pp. 233-234.
42 *Ibid.*, p. 237.

FOOTNOTES TO MIRANDA *(Continued)*

43 *Ibid.*, p. 238.
44 *Ibid.*, p. 240.
45 *Ibid.*, p. 241.
46 *Ibid.*, pp. 252-253.
47 *Ibid.*, p. 259.
48 *Ibid.*, p. 264.
49 *Ibid.*, p. 264.
50 Katherine Anne Porter, *The Days Before,* "Portrait: Old South," p. 155.
51 *Ibid.*, pp. 155-161.

FOOTNOTES TO THE NOVELETTES

52 Edmund Wilson, *Classics and Commercials,* p. 222.
53 Katherine Anne Porter, *The Leaning Tower and Other Stories,* "The Leaning Tower," p. 159.
54 *Ibid.*, p. 160.
55 *Ibid.*, p. 161.
56 *Ibid.*, p. 162.
57 *Ibid.*, p. 149.
58 *Ibid.*, p. 178.
59 *Ibid.*, pp. 194-195.
60 *Ibid.*, p. 197.
61 *Ibid.*, p. 234.
62 *Ibid.*, pp. 244-245.
63 Katherine Anne Porter, *Pale Horse, Pale Rider,* "Noon Wine," p. 127.
64 *Ibid.*, p. 130.
65 *Ibid.*, p. 147.
66 *Ibid.*, pp. 152-153.
67 *Ibid.*, pp. 162-163.
68 *Ibid.*, p. 168.
69 *Ibid.*, pp. 174-175.
70 *Ibid.*, pp. 175-176.
71 Katherine Anne Porter, *Flowering Judas and Other Stories* (New York, 1935), "The Cracked Looking-Glass," pp. 215-216.
72 *Ibid.*, pp. 218-219.

FOOTNOTES TO THE SHORT STORIES

73 Katherine Anne Porter, *Flowering Judas and Other Stories,* "Maria Concepcion," p. 35.
74 Katherine Anne Porter, *Flowering Judas and Other Stories,* "The Jilting of Granny Weatherall," p. 131.
75 *Ibid.*, p. 136.
76 Katherine Anne Porter, *The Leaning Tower and Other Stories,* "The Downward Path to Wisdom," p. 83.
77 *Ibid.*, p. 82.
78 *Ibid.*, pp. 105-106.
79 *Ibid.*, pp. 110-111.

BIBLIOGRAPHY

Hyman, Stanley Edgar, *The Armed Vision*, New York, Alfred A. Knopf, 1948.

James, Henry, *The Art of the Novel*, New York, Scribners, 1953.

Porter, Katherine Anne, *Flowering Judas and Other Stories*, New York, Harcourt, Brace, 1935.

Porter, Katherine Anne, *Pale Horse, Pale Rider*, New York, Harcourt, Brace, 1939.

Porter, Katherine Anne, *The Days Before*, New York, Harcourt, Brace, 1952.

Porter, Katherine Anne, *The Leaning Tower and Other Stories*, New York, Harcourt, Brace, 1944.

Van Gelder, Robert, *The New York Times Book Review*, April 14, 1940, reprinted in *Writers and Writing*, New York, Scribners, 1945.

Wilson, Edmund, reprinted in *Classics and Commercials*, New York, Farrar, Straus, 1950.